CHAD HARRINGTON

YOUR

Spiritual Formation

PLAN

*A Devotional Workbook
to Guide Your Next
Steps with God*

Your Spiritual Formation Plan
Copyright © 2021 by Chad Harrington

Requests for information should be sent via email to HIM Publications. Visit www.himpublications.com for contact information.

All Scripture quotations, unless otherwise indicated, are taken from the Holy Bible, New International Version®, NIV®. Copyright © 1973, 1978, 1984 by Biblica, Inc.® Used by permission of Zondervan. All rights reserved worldwide. www.zondervan.com. The "NIV" and "New International Version" are trademarks registered in the United States Patent and Trademark Office by Biblica, Inc.®

Scripture quotations marked NRSV are taken from the New Revised Standard Version Bible. Copyright © 1989 National Council of the Churches of Christ in the United States of America. Used by permission. All rights reserved worldwide.

Scripture quotations marked ESV are taken from the ESV® Bible (The Holy Bible, English Standard Version®). Copyright © 2001 by Crossway, a publishing ministry of Good News Publishers. Used by permission. All rights reserved.

Scripture quotations marked KJV are taken from the King James Version of the Holy Bible.

Emphases in Scripture quotations are the author's.

All rights reserved. No part of this book, including icons and images, may be reproduced in any manner without prior written permission from the copyright holder.

ISBN: 978-1-970102-44-4 (Paperback)
ISBN: 978-1-970102-45-1 (Kindle)
ISBN: 978-1-970102-46-8 (ePub)

Cover and interior design: Harrington Interactive Media (harringtoninteractive.com)

Printed in the United States of America

himpublications.com

CONTENTS

How to Use This Workbook 5

PART 1: Your Initial Spiritual Formation Plan 9
    1. Introducing the Rule of Life 11
    2. Crafting Your Rule of Life 13
    3. Identifying Your Greatest Desire 19
    4. Identifying Your Greatest Barriers 23

PART 2: Your Next Steps in the Disciplines 29
    5. Introducing the Disciplines 31
    6. The 21-Day Challenge 35
    7. Solitude 39
    8. Silence 43
    9. Rest 49
    10. Reading Scripture 55
    11. Prayer 61
    12. Fasting 67
    13. Service 73
    14. Submission 79
    15. Confession 85
    16. Listening 89
    17. Refining Your Rule of Life 93

PART 3: Your Next Season of Spiritual Formation 97
    18. A Seasonal Approach to Spiritual Formation 99
    19. Planning Your Next Season 103

Appendix A: Rule of Life Examples...113
Appendix B: How to Do a Book Study..117
Appendix C: Key Scripture Verses for Memorization..............123
Notes..125
About the Author..127

HOW TO USE THIS WORKBOOK

My spiritual formation journey picked up speed when I repented of my sin in a fresh way and sought God when I was just a boy. God got ahold of my heart early and changed my life. Even in my adolescence, God used some of the core disciplines in this book to shape me, the effects of which I still carry with me today. My parents had laid the groundwork, and God used that foundation and a handful of other people to jumpstart my early experiences with God.

> It was God himself who formed me.

In the time since my early experiences, as God has continued to form me—and even put up with me—I've compiled lessons along the way, and this workbook contains some of the most important ones I've learned thus far on my spiritual formation journey.

I wrote this workbook for disciples of Jesus at all points in their walk: from the new Christian to the pastor of a church, from the young disciple to the seasoned disciple-maker. It's for any follower of Jesus who wants to experience the fullness of God in a fresh way. In Christ we "have been given fullness," but we are still encouraged to "press on toward the goal to win the prize" for which God has called us "heavenward in Christ Jesus" (Col. 2:10; Phil. 3:14). The exercises in this workbook can help any disciple grow.

Why I Wrote This

The goal of this workbook is to help you take your next steps with God. I share lessons I've learned and offer prompts to help you determine your course of action each step of the way. My hope is that, by the grace of God, you can use this resource to make progress on your spiritual formation journey.

The devotional material in these pages was birthed from my personal experiences and from my interactions with students as I've taught spiritual formation in my church. The first time I taught a class on spiritual formation, I created the first iteration of this workbook so everyone could walk away with a customized plan. The people in that class and those in the young adults' group I was leading found value in what I created, so I expanded that first iteration into what you're holding now. I saw how it helped people to put their plan on paper, so I wanted to make it available to even more people and churches. May you benefit from this workbook as others have.

Three Important Influences

As I wrote the devotionals for this workbook and created prompts, three major influences formed my thinking. First, Dallas Willard's books have made a profound impact on my life in general, but one book in particular inspired me to think in terms of crafting a literal plan. In his book *The Spirit of the Disciplines*, he writes about the reality that we are called to obey all of Christ's commands, as Jesus made clear in the Great Commission. Then, Willard pushes the idea further to say that we need *a plan* in order for this happen. His statement about planning for spiritual formation should capture our attention: "It is the rare leader or teacher today who can calmly say, 'Here's how you do it,' and state specific tried and true steps actually accessible to the earnest inquirer." I've found this to be true, even today. This workbook doesn't contain *the way* for planning spiritual formation, but it serves as *a way* to help others start a workable plan toward obedience to all of Jesus' commands.

The second influence that drives the content of this workbook is the idea that spiritual disciplines are God's "means of grace"—ways through which God pours out his grace into our lives. Spiritual formation happens as we practice spiritual disciplines, and these disciplines are key ways we receive blessings from God. The practices I encourage in this book are channels through which God floods us with his overwhelming grace. This grace, poured out through the Holy Spirit, changes our hearts and lives as we participate with God through our actions. We're set free to run hard after God, the benefit of which is "holiness, and the result is eternal life" (Rom. 6:22).

The third influence is something I learned through personal experience: spiritual formation is a journey that requires time, training, and experimentation. This workbook presents a unique opportunity to experiment and play as you make plans for your journey. What drives this work-in-progress mentality is the idea that we grow by experimenting with spiritual disciplines. The idea of "experimenting" with anything usually connotes bad behavior, but we ought to change that! When we experiment in good ways with pure hearts before the Lord, it's difficult to go very wrong, especially if we're humble and experiment in community and in constant communication with God. I emphasize experimentation here because many of the exercises in this workbook assume you're willing to put yourself out there and try new practices. In the pages that follow, I ask you to put pen to paper, brainstorm, and play with ideas, and for some of you this might feel uncomfortable. But if you can bear some momentary discomfort, you will grow stronger in the end.

Three Companion Resources

HIM Publications recorded and released the class I originally taught that goes with this workbook. It's now available as a video course called *Spiritual Formation*. So while this workbook can serve as a stand-alone resource, it's not a complete guide to spiritual formation. I've written it with the assumption that you'll use other resources as well. I recommend you utilize my video course—to hear more of my heart for each part of the plan—and at least one other book.

My *Spiritual Formation* video course provides more substantive teaching on spiritual formation as a whole and on the specific disciplines in this workbook. Learn more and sign up at himpublications.com/spiritual. Dallas Willard's *Renovation of the Heart: Putting on the Character of Christ* is the main text I reference in my course, and I highly recommend this book for its depth and insight into how spiritual formation works. Those are my top two recommendations to you because this workbook was created with those in mind. If you watch the spiritual formation video sessions and read *Renovation of the Heart*, you'll be well suited for making good progress on your spiritual formation journey.

A third resource I recommend for going deeper into the specific disciplines of this workbook is *Celebration of Discipline: The Path to Spiritual Growth* by Richard J. Foster. This is considered the gold standard for introducing the spiritual disciplines to modern readers. It covers all the core disciplines included in this book.

At the end of most chapters, I offer other supplemental resources for the subject matter of that chapter. These recommended resources can make up for what is lacking in my short devotionals. The devotional thoughts are intentionally short because the goal of this resource is primarily about taking action. I don't provide in this workbook the necessary biblical theology, background, or thorough treatment each discipline deserves, as do the above resources. It builds on those materials by helping you make plans and take specific actions.

Three Sections of This Workbook

What follows will form your spiritual formation plan in three parts. I've included checkboxes throughout the workbook to help you track your progress on the journey. For each chapter, you will take specific steps.

- Part 1, "Your Initial Spiritual Formation Plan," jumpstarts your journey with the most important task of the whole workbook: crafting your Rule of Life. It also guides you to determine your greatest desire and your most pressing challenges right now.
- Part 2, "Your Next Steps in the Disciplines," introduces the disciplines, encourages you to take the 21-Day Challenge, and helps you formulate initial plans for ten core disciplines.
- Part 3, "Your Next Season of Spiritual Formation," helps you build on your plan from the first two parts and apply your foundation toward a long-term approach to formation.

A final suggestion before you jump in: go at your own pace. Allow this workbook to push you, but if push comes to shove, pause and evaluate your pace. I've seen how easily people get overwhelmed as they form their plan, so remember that at any point, you can pause, go backwards, speed up, or do whatever you need to do in order to complete this workbook successfully. And remember:

> God's grace abounds, and his grace is the air we breathe as we walk along the Way.

So press on with the confidence that God leads disciples of Jesus in and through his abounding grace.

Part 1

YOUR INITIAL SPIRITUAL FORMATION PLAN

Part 1 helps you form the foundation for your spiritual formation plan. Learn the value of creating a Rule of Life, how it functions in your plan, and how to create yours. Then, identify your single greatest desire in life right now so you can proceed in authenticity. The last chapter in this part helps you identify your greatest barriers to connecting with God right now.

1

INTRODUCING THE RULE OF LIFE

Your Rule of Life lays the foundation of your entire spiritual formation plan, and it is the most important exercise of the whole workbook. When you're done, you'll walk away with a clear vision—on paper—of who you want to be in Christ. This is an important exercise because it sets the course of your spiritual formation journey and helps you keep your way. Let me share with you what it is, some background behind it, and how to create one.

We make resolutions for the year, goals for the day, and plans for the grocery store, but what about plans for our lives as a whole? The Rule of Life helps us take a macro-view of our lives and state exactly who we want to be. Some Christians push back at this point and say, "I know who I am in Christ, *according to Scripture*." I respond by saying, "That's good!" We need to know our identity in Christ. But this exercise goes beyond our general identity in Christ as outlined in Scripture and into our unique identities. Your Rule captures your unique identity in light of your general identity as a disciple of Christ Jesus. Here's how I define the Rule of Life:

> Your Rule of Life is a high-level overview of who you want to be in Christ within your personality.

The tradition of crafting a Rule of Life goes back to Saint Benedict in the sixth century. Saint Benedict was a Christian monk who wanted to codify his vision for the community he led. They knew their general identity in Christ, but Saint Benedict wanted to shape his community by putting on paper the unique characteristics he envisioned for their community. It became known as *The Rule of Saint Benedict*. Since that time, many people have adopted this practice for not only their community but also for their personal lives.

As you craft your own, it's important to understand what the Rule of Life is not. The word "rule" does not mean creating *rules* for yourself. Instead the word means more like creating *the ruler* of your life: a tool for measuring where you are on your journey of discipleship in light of where you want to be. This is different than goal-setting or making New Year's resolutions because those contain time-bound goals (which serve a different function than the Rule). Neither is the Rule of Life a new "law" for yourself to earn status with God. It's simply the standard of life you want to live before God in Christ.

In the next section, I describe how to craft your Rule, but let me pause to offer a few pieces of advice based on my experience writing my own Rule and guiding others to write theirs. My first piece of advice is to have fun with this exercise. It's an exciting step! Hopefully you will go back to your Rule time and time again throughout your life, and this begins your process toward that end. Second, while I advise you to solidify your Rule at some point, plan to make changes to your initial draft. In fact, drafting multiple times is a necessary part of this process. Don't worry too much about "getting it perfect" the first time.

My last piece of advice is to keep the goal of love in mind. The long-standing tradition of crafting a Rule of Life exists ultimately to help you love God with all your whole heart, soul, and strength, and to love others too. If at any point you find your Rule does not help you love God and others, then you should change it to become something that does—or else abandon the practice all together. Remember that the ultimate goal is love.

2

CRAFTING YOUR RULE OF LIFE

> In this chapter you will:
> - ☐ Choose the style of your Rule of Life.
> - ☐ Draft your Rule of Life.

Below are step-by-step instructions on how to craft your Rule of Life prayerfully. Remember, you're creating *a draft*, and you can change it afterwards. Don't get bogged down by trying to get everything perfect the first time. The most important task here is simply to get started. The pages at the end of this chapter offer you space to draft your Rule.

Set aside an hour or two to complete your first draft. Write without analyzing what you're writing. If you're not sure about something, go ahead and jot it down anyway. You can edit or delete later. Allow yourself to go with the flow. This is especially important for more analytical people. If you're more of a go-with-the-flow, spontaneous person, your challenge might be to complete this first draft at all! That's why I recommend setting aside a few hours in which you can start and finish this initial draft.

Aim to fill up an entire page or two. You can use the outline I provide below—which comprises spirit, mind, body, and social aspects of life—but don't feel bound by that structure. Perhaps you want to organize your Rule of Life in a different way and use another piece of paper or a journal. That's perfectly fine! You might organize your Rule of Life in terms of daily, weekly, monthly, quarterly, and annual rhythms, for example. Or you might organize it based on your mission, vision, roles, gifts, and relationships.

I offer a four-part outline here because the specific divisions have helped me think in holistic terms about who I want to be. Plus, they're based on the four core parts of who we are as people: spirit, mind, body, and social. I've adapted their meanings from Dallas Willard's *Renovation of the Heart* (with examples in italics):

SPIRIT: The heart and will that form the character of our lives.
Example: "I will seek a heart of compassion."

MIND: The thoughts and feelings of our lives.
Example: "I will reject thoughts of guilt, shame, and regret."

BODY: Our bodies, God's temple.
Example: "I will work out three times a week for at least fifteen minutes."

SOCIAL: The people in our lives.
Example: "I will be honest and transparent in my relationships."

For more examples, see Appendix A.

One final tip before you get started: While I recommend drafting this in one sitting, you may need more time. Regardless of how many times you sit down to work on it, it's important to finish your first draft completely *within one week*. Make that your aim!

The following steps will guide you as you write your first draft.

1. Go to a quiet place where you can write and be alone with God. Bring with you pen and paper (or use the space in this workbook).
2. Start by asking God what he wants your life to look like in general.
3. Then ask God specific, open-ended questions for each area on the list: *What do you want of me in this area? And in that area?* Write what comes to mind. It's okay to write something, even if the idea might be yours and not directly from God speaking to you on a certain point.
4. In a similar way, ask yourself who you uniquely want to be within your personality for each area: *How do I want to live? What's important to me in this area?* Write those things down as bullet-point phrases or sentences. If you prefer bullets, start each bullet with "To . . ." or if you decide to use complete sentences, start each one with "I will . . ."
5. After you go through each aspect, ask both yourself and God: *Am I missing anything important in any area?*

That's it! By taking those steps, you've completed your first draft. While you may add items later and tweak your Rule as you progress through this workbook, don't worry about modifying it until the very end. Once you've completed the exercises in the pages that follow, you will have a fuller sense of what you want your life to look like as a whole. At that point, you will be able to redraft your Rule and begin solidifying it into the document that can serve you for a lifetime.

> ## Supplemental Reading
>
> Go deeper into this topic with Stephen A. Macchia's book *Crafting a Rule of Life: An Invitation to the Well-Ordered Way* (Downers Grove: IVP, 2012). While my instructions here offer what you need for crafting your Rule of Life, this book provides more in-depth instructions.

SPIRIT: The heart and will that form the character of my life.

MIND: The thoughts and feelings of my life.

BODY: My body, God's temple.

SOCIAL: The people in my life.

3

IDENTIFYING YOUR GREATEST DESIRE

In this chapter you will:

☐ Identify your desires in life right now.
☐ Land on your primary desire.

Now that you've completed the initial draft of your Rule of Life, you're ready to identify your greatest desire in life right now. In this chapter, I address desire in general, then guide you to pick your number-one greatest desire.

What you want carries important implications for determining the shape of your life. Clearly naming what you want matters. After all, when Jesus walked the earth, he asked people about their desires. For example, two of John the Baptist's disciples began trailing Jesus near the Jordan River. Jesus asked them, "What do you want?" They replied, "Where are you staying?" (John 1:37–38). Apparently, all they wanted was to spend time with Jesus! So Jesus spent the rest of the day with them because that's what they wanted.

In a different time and place, Jesus asked a woman—the mother of James and John—about her desire. Jesus was traveling to Jerusalem with his twelve disciples, and she approached Jesus for a favor. Jesus said, "What is it you want?" She said, "Grant that one of these two sons of mine may sit at your right and the other at your left in your kingdom" (Matt. 20:21). She wanted her sons to have top positions of power in his kingdom.

In the very next section of Matthew's Gospel, we see yet another example. Jesus was leaving Jericho with his disciples, and two blind men sitting on the side of the road cried out to him. The crowd tried to quiet them, so they shouted all the more! Jesus stopped walking and asked them, "What do you want me to do for you?" They replied, "We want our sight" (Matt. 20:32–33).

> The Gospels make it clear that Jesus cared about people's desires while he was on earth.

It's not just in the Gospels, though. Throughout Scripture God shows interest in what people want—at least as a starting place on their journey. The same is true today. God doesn't always give us what we want, because our desire might not be his desire for us. But God generally wants to know what we want, because we're his children and he cares about us.

What do you want right now? Perhaps you want a new job, a break from your current situation in life, or deeper friendships. As you answer this question at the end of this chapter, name what you want in general *right now*. And don't worry about how "spiritual" your answer might be. Too often we separate our regular lives from our spiritual lives, as if we could compartmentalize our lives.

Perhaps you struggle to know what you want because you're used to thinking about what you *should* want, not what you *actually* want. With all of life's obligations, you've stopped asking what you want. Your desires don't matter because *only what God wants* matters. Yet as seen in the Gospels, Jesus asked people what *they wanted*. God's desire for you is perfect, but sometimes God's desire for you is not that different from your own. Putting your desire in a category of "good" or "bad" is not the point of naming your primary desire.

Naming what we want in life right now helps us live authentically, even if our current desire doesn't align with the type of desires we want to have one day. While it might feel counterintuitive, we can more effectively seek what God wants for us when we name our own desire because we're living from where we actually are, not where we feel we should be.

Perhaps your desire is directly "spiritual," and you want to connect with God through prayer, for example. Write that down as your primary desire. But maybe your desire isn't so spiritual, yet it's your real desire in life right now. You want to find a spouse or to have children or to be successful in your career or to find rest finally. Whatever your desire, name it. There's room in your relationship with God for your true self. In fact, honestly naming your primary desire is an important step toward making real progress in your spiritual formation journey.

Also, make sure to name your *primary* desire. As people we have many desires, but you should name only one. Consider how your life is like a story. Compelling stories contain characters who are driven by a single desire. Other desires they may have don't drive them like their primary desire. This is your life's story, so pick only one desire to help your plot develop.

> **Supplemental Reading**
>
> David G. Benner's *Desiring God's Will: Aligning Our Hearts with the Heart of God* (Downers Grove: IVP, 2005) offers a strong theology of desire. He rightly focuses on God's will and desire but does so in a way that takes into account our will and desire as people too.

Brainstorm about your single greatest desire below. Start by listing all the desires that come to mind, then look over your list and land on just one. This can be challenging, but you can do it!

What are your desires in life right now?

_____
_____
_____
_____
_____
_____
_____
_____
_____
_____
_____
_____
_____

Of these, what is your *number-one desire*?

_____
_____
_____
_____
_____

4

IDENTIFYING YOUR GREATEST BARRIERS

> In this chapter you will:
> - ☐ Identify your greatest surface-level barrier.
> - ☐ Identify your greatest heart-level barrier.

The relational goal of spiritual formation is union with God. In our journey toward union, though, we will face significant barriers. These barriers come from other people, from ourselves, and even from our Great Enemy. Since we're in a battle for our souls, precisely identifying our greatest challenges is important.

> What is your greatest barrier right now?

At any given point in your journey toward union with God, one challenge gets in your way more than any other challenge. That's what this chapter helps you identify. When I ask people about their greatest barrier without providing any sort of parameters or qualifications, people almost always mention a surface-level barrier at first. It's something like *busyness, distraction,* or *not knowing how to take the next step*. These are real barriers, but they're more on the practical side of the issue. There's always something deeper under the surface.

I've learned to make space not only for surface-level barriers but also for heart-level barriers. The truth is that we're up against both kinds of barriers in our journey: surface-level barriers, which we can more easily identify, and deeper, heart-level barriers, which require more effort to identify. Deep, heart-level barriers keep us from God and often connect to the root cause of a sin struggle, for example. Other examples of heart-level barriers include an incomplete understanding of the gospel, unresolved hurt or anger, or abiding issues of guilt and shame. Sometimes we're unaware of these deep barriers in our lives, so we might need more time to discern what they are. In this chapter, you'll have an opportunity to answer questions about your surface and heart barriers.

Answering these questions requires vulnerability, humility, and hope. When we honestly share our struggles, we expose our hearts—to ourselves, to God, and perhaps to a trusted mentor or friend. And most people don't typically admit a problem unless they are certain of a possible solution. Take heart because our hope is in Jesus Christ, and in Christ is no condemnation because the Spirit sets us free (Rom. 8:1–2). As we look at challenges that lie before us, remember this truth:

> Jesus is our solution, our hope, and our victory!

As you start this exercise, begin with your greatest surface-level barrier. Then, ask yourself what might be the underlying barrier at the heart level. Often the two barriers connect, such as the root and fruit of a tree. Think of the surface-level barrier as a clue to what's happening at the heart level.

Supplemental Reading

Bill Hull's book *Conversion and Discipleship: You Can't Have One Without the Other* (Grand Rapids: Zondervan, 2016) contains a very helpful section on the topic of heart-level barriers: Chapter 1, "The Gospel." He identifies six false gospels people commonly believe. Knowing these false gospels can help those who want to go deeper into how our understanding of how the gospel affects our lives.

Identifying Your Greatest Barriers

In the space below, list out the different barriers that come to mind as you think and pray. Then, pick one surface-level barrier and one heart-level barrier.

What surface-level barriers exist between you and God right now?

_____
_____
_____
_____
_____
_____
_____
_____
_____
_____
_____
_____
_____

From that list, what is the *single greatest* surface-level barrier for you? This is usually something simple and practical (perhaps your initial thought when you began brainstorming).

_____
_____
_____
_____
_____

What might be at the root of your greatest surface-level barrier? List any heart-level barriers that come to mind.

_____
_____
_____
_____
_____
_____
_____
_____
_____
_____

What is the greatest heart-level barrier keeping you from connecting with God right now?

_____
_____
_____
_____
_____

Spiritual Formation Video Course

You've now completed Part 1! You drafted your Rule of Life and named your greatest desire and barriers. Before you start Part 2, I want to remind you of my *Spiritual Formation* video course, which goes with this workbook. It's available to you for on-demand streaming at himpublications.com/spiritual.

In this course, I offer in-depth teaching on the topics of this workbook. It provides twelve hours of content, which gives you a more holistic understanding of spiritual formation. For each discipline, I unpack key Scripture passages, apply their meaning, and connect each session to exercises in this workbook. The course is designed to help you go deeper into spiritual formation.

Register at
himpublications.com/spiritual

Part 2

YOUR NEXT STEPS IN THE DISCIPLINES

Part 2 builds on Part 1 by helping you take initial steps in specific disciplines. Take a bird's eye view of some core disciplines, then dive into one specific discipline with the 21-Day Challenge. The remainder of this section will guide you through establishing disciplines that help launch you into cultivating lifelong spiritual formation habits.

5

INTRODUCING THE DISCIPLINES

> In this chapter you will:
> ☐ Identify the spiritual discipline in which you have the most experience.
> ☐ Identify a discipline in which you most want to grow.

We all yearn for connection with God. But how do we go about pursuing this relationship with him? How can we cultivate a close relationship with *the creator of the universe*? Doing this seems high and lofty, no doubt, but throughout history—typified by the life of Jesus Christ—we're given specific ways through which we can predictably connect with God. Jesus encouraged us to "ask, seek, and knock" in our pursuit of God, and Scripture confirms that God "rewards those who earnestly seek him" (Matt. 7:7–8; Heb. 11:6). Together these passages mean it's possible to seek and find God. God's not elusive! He wants us to know him and to be known by him, and he's provided clear avenues through which we can do just that. These are the spiritual disciplines.

In the introduction to this workbook, I referred to the spiritual disciplines as "means of grace." This phrase puts the emphasis on God's work in us, even though we cooperate with him.

> Spiritual formation happens at the convergence of our pursuit of him and his pursuit of us.

But God's grace comes before anything we ever do. Plus, his grace carries us to completion. That's why it's helpful to talk about the disciplines in terms of the means of God's grace.

The catch, though, is we do not take the back seat but actively "participate in the divine nature" (2 Pet. 1:4). Our participation with God comes through these means of grace—these channels, these disciplines, these means through which God pours out his blessings. They require discipline and effort on our part, even though our efforts are energized by God. Dallas Willard brings all this together in one sentence:

> "Grace is opposed to earning, not to effort."

We exert effort through the disciplines, but God does the actual work of transformation in us. Jesus said, "Apart from me you can do nothing" (John 15:5). I believe the opposite is true too, though: if we can't do anything apart from Jesus, then with Jesus we can do much! Paul describes this interactive relationship in terms of our labor and God's energy: "I labor, struggling with all his energy, which so powerfully works in me" (Col. 1:29). We expel God's energy in us through the disciplines, which are God's chosen means through which he's appointed us to do much in our lives—and through our lives.

Think of the disciplines as oases in the desert. If someone is wandering in the desert looking for water, an oasis provides the water they need. As a result, the wanderer can come to that oasis, and other oases they might find, in order to satiate their thirst. These oases in the desert become reliable sources of life for them.

God calls himself "the spring of living water," and we find his grace pouring out in specific places (Jer. 2:13; see also John 4:14). These places—these oases in the desert—give us unique access to his grace, and if we go to them for life, we can reliably expect to be filled up by his grace. This doesn't mean we always feel God's presence, but we know God has and always will meet us in the disciplines. They are oases in the desert. Even if the rewards Jesus promised us are not immediate, we can rely on the truth of his Word to sustain us through difficult or seemingly dry seasons. We don't lose heart when the disciplines become difficult; instead, we keep faith, trusting that the author and perfector of our faith will see us through as he reigns from the "right hand of the throne of God" (Heb. 12:2).

I've adapted the list of disciplines below from Dallas Willard's list of key disciplines from his book *The Spirit of the Disciplines*. My goal by listing them here is to help you get an overview of spiritual disciplines before stepping into specific ones. They're divided into disciplines of abstinence and disciplines of engagement because the formation journey includes both abstaining from and engaging in certain activities in order to grow in the likeness of Christ. Additional disciplines certainly exist, but these disciplines are key ones to get you started thinking about the disciplines as a whole (*disciplines covered in this workbook have an asterisk).

Key Disciplines of Abstinence

Solitude*	Matthew 4:1; Mark 1:35; John 6:15
Silence*	Proverbs 10:19; Mark 14:60–61; James 1:19–20
Rest*	Exodus 16:23–30; Deuteronomy 5:12; Matthew 12:1–8
Fasting*	Isaiah 58:3, 6–9; Matthew 4:1–11; Acts 13:2–3
Frugality	Romans 13:8; 1 Timothy 6:17–18; James 5:1–5
Chastity	Matthew 19:11–12; 1 Corinthians 6:18
Secrecy	Matthew 6:1–18; Mark 7:24
Sacrifice	1 Chronicles 21:20–26; Luke 12:2–4; Romans 12:1–2

Key Disciplines of Engagement

Reading Scripture*	Psalm 1:1–6; Matthew 4:4; Ephesians 5:25–26
Prayer*	Matthew 6:5–13; Mark 1:35; Acts 10:1–9
Service*	Matthew 20:25–28; John 13:14; Colossians 3:22–24
Submission*	Luke 2:51; Hebrews 13:7; Ephesians 5:21; 1 Peter 5:5
Confession*	Leviticus 16:21; Matthew 3:6; James 5:16
Listening*	Proverbs 15:22; Mark 4:9; James 1:19
Worship	Isaiah 6:1–3; Acts 13:1–3; Revelation 5:12–13
Celebration	Ecclesiastes 5:18–20; John 2:1–11; Luke 15:23
Fellowship	Acts 2:42; 1 Corinthians 12:7–11; 1 John 1:3

With which discipline do you have the most experience?

_____

In which discipline are you the most interested to grow?

_____

6

THE 21-DAY CHALLENGE

In this chapter you will:
- ☐ Pick your micro-discipline for the challenge.
- ☐ Ask a friend to join you.
- ☐ Choose an end date.
- ☐ Get started!

Now that you have an overview of the disciplines, it's time to jump into action! We'll go through the core disciplines, starting in the next chapter, but we learn best when we combine our knowledge *with action*. Taking action is vital from the beginning to the end of our discipleship journey. We can only learn to walk in step with the Holy Spirit if we're actually moving and taking steps at all. That's why I created the 21-Day Challenge. This challenge gives you a jumpstart on your spiritual formation journey.

> The 21-Day Challenge is to pick a single discipline and practice that discipline every day for twenty-one days straight.

Practice a discipline of your choice as best you currently know how. It's not about "getting it right," but about starting small. The purpose is to help you grow in developing spiritual habits. My hope is that you will also gain confidence in what God can do in you as you follow through with your intentions.

Beginning to build your spiritual muscles early in the discipleship process is important because it reminds you that it's about progress not perfection, and learning as you go instead of focusing on "arriving." As disciples of Jesus, we're in this race for the long haul, not just a sprint. So my goal is to help you cultivate lifelong habits, starting with simple ones. If you're already experienced in the disciplines, the 21-Day Challenge is your opportunity to restart a habit, explore a discipline less familiar to you, or expand your current habits in a fresh way. Using the two lists of key disciplines from the last chapter, select *just one discipline* and focus on it for the next three weeks.

Practice that one discipline, and here's a piece of advice: choose a "microform" of that discipline. For example, if you choose the discipline of reading Scripture and you're rusty, then read the Bible for only a small amount of time each day or meditate on a small portion of the Word—whatever is doable for you. If you choose prayer, you might decide to pray the Our Father Prayer (also known as the Lord's Prayer) every day. Perhaps you'd like to fast for one meal a day for twenty-one days or silence your phone for a window of time each day.

> Download a printable PDF of the Our Father Prayer by going to himpublications.com/father.

Whatever you choose, follow through with your commitment for the next twenty-one days in a row. Here's the kicker: start today! There's no need to wait another day to take your next step.

While I intentionally chose the number of days for this challenge, nothing special about twenty-one days influenced my decision. It's long enough to stretch a person but not too long to push them too hard. While this exercise may expose a weakness or two you didn't know you had, you should also experience breakthroughs, waves of refreshment, and excitement about moving forward with this and other disciplines. If at any point you want to give up, I encourage you to press on and perhaps modify your commitment, rather than abandoning the challenge altogether.

I hope you also know yourself better by the end of the next three weeks. Self-knowledge, surprisingly enough, is very important in our spiritual journey. When we're aware of both our abilities and our weaknesses, our awareness helps us form workable plans for ourselves that lead to real growth rather than mere wishful thinking. Then, as we grow, what was once difficult becomes easier. Proper self-knowledge helps us reasonably and successfully submit to God's work in our lives.

Another important outcome I hope you gain from this exercise is your growth in integrity. Integrity in the context of spiritual formation means we follow through with our commitments. If we say we're going to do something, let's do it! Living with integrity means we're true to ourselves before God. Jesus described integrity like this: "Simply let your 'Yes' be 'Yes,' and your 'No,' 'No'; anything beyond this comes from the evil one" (Matt. 5:37). The 21-Day Challenge creates space for cultivating integrity as it offers a practical way to say yes—*or no*—to yourself before God. So make a small commitment and stick to it as best you can.

Saying no and sticking to that is just as important as saying yes and sticking to it. We can easily overextend ourselves and overcommit, especially at the outset of a new challenge. But as we learn to let our yes be yes and our no be no, we allow space for God to build integrity in us. In this way, we work with God as he forms and substantiates our character. God works in our hearts and through our actions to make us more whole and holy before him.

Here are two tips for success in this challenge. First, while you're obviously free to do more than one discipline, *commit to only one discipline for the 21-Day Challenge.* That way you can make sure to follow through with that one, even if all else fails. Second, and this can make it more fun, ask a friend or a mentor to join you. You will likely pick a different discipline than your companion, but start and end on the same day together. Complete the exercise below, tell your friend what you're doing (even though you don't have it all figured out), and invite them to join you. Then, go ahead—pick up that phone, send that text message, or initiate that conversation—and get started today! This provides some built-in accountability and encouragement so you can make sure to cross the finish line of this challenge.

> ## Supplemental Reading
>
> Caroline Leaf is a Christian and a communication pathologist and audiologist. She combined her understanding of Scripture with how the brain works in her book *Switch on Your Brain: The Key to Peak Happiness, Thinking, and Health* (Grand Rapids: Baker, 2013). Her research encourages readers that their brain can change, and her book features a 21-day "brain detox plan," which provides additional perspective for the 21-Day Challenge.

Your Spiritual Formation Plan

Use the space below to plan your 21-Day Challenge.

Which discipline would you like to commit to for the next twenty-one days, starting today? What will it look like for you to follow through with this discipline?

_____
_____
_____
_____
_____
_____
_____
_____
_____

How will you measure success at the end of this challenge? Describe at least one *minimum measurable parameter* of success here.

_____
_____
_____
_____
_____

Whom will you ask to join you? This can be a family member, a friend, or a mentor.

_____

What is the end date for your challenge? Put that date in your calendar or post it somewhere as a reminder.

_____

7

SOLITUDE

> In this chapter you will:
> ☐ Choose your time and place for regular solitude.
> ☐ Choose your time and place for your next retreat.

Now that you had an intro into the disciplines and you got your feet wet, it's time to walk through some core disciplines—starting with solitude. Why start here? In *The Spirit of the Disciplines*, Willard calls solitude the "most fundamental" discipline of abstinence. Solitude is more than just getting away from other people, though; it's withdrawing from the world *to be with God*. God's presence separates solitude from isolation because:

> Solitude builds us up, and isolation breaks us down.

When we pursue solitude, we join the ranks of the heroes of the faith such as Joseph, David, Elijah, Paul, John—and most important of all, Jesus. Jesus sought solitude at important junctures in his ministry. Right after his baptism, for example, he spent forty days in the desert in extended solitude (Matt. 4:1–11; Luke 4:1–13). Then, just before he designated twelve of his disciples as apostles, he went to a mountainside alone to pray (Luke 6:12).

He also made space for solitude in short intervals of everyday life: an hour here, an afternoon there. On one such occasion, "Very early in the morning, while it was still dark, Jesus got up, left the house and went off to a solitary place, where he prayed." He found solitude after a night of intense ministry, during which the whole town had come to him and he healed many sick people (Mark 1:35). Scripture makes it clear that Jesus regularly sought solitude (Luke 5:16).

One particular retreat Jesus took piques our curiosity about him: In John 6, the large crowds Jesus had fed started to make arrangements for him to become king. But, it says, "Jesus, knowing that they intended to come and make him king by force, *withdrew again to a mountain by himself*" (John 6:15). Why did he withdraw from the crowds? Why didn't he teach them more truth, spend more time with them, or receive his rightful crown? We don't know the exact reason for his withdrawal. Perhaps he wanted to focus on his true identity and on the Father's timing on all matters of kingship. While the cause of his retreat remains a mystery, we know he got away to be alone. Solitude was important to Jesus.

Like Jesus, we need to find solitude for both short and long periods of time. We need regular time each week, sometimes on a daily basis, for solitude. We might snag five minutes here, thirty minutes there, or perhaps even hours at a time (depending on our season of life). We also need periodic "retreats" to be alone for days at a time. To go on a retreat means to get away from your regular environment for an extended period of time to be alone with God. If you've never been on a retreat, go! This practice could lead to significant breakthroughs in your life. I know retreats have led to breakthroughs in my life.

> Let me issue a challenge to you: make a weekly habit of regular solitude and a yearly habit of going on an extended retreat.

For your extended retreat, take three to five days where you get away to be alone with God. Your ability to get away like this depends on your season of life, your means, and the availability of retreat centers. And if you can't find a retreat center for this, a hotel, cabin, or house rental can work just fine. The most important thing is to make space for true solitude and to find a quiet place away from your home. How else will you connect with God at a heart level if you don't seek solitude to be alone with him?

Solitude forms each of us differently, and the nature of solitude changes during different seasons of our journey. Early in my walk with God, regular and lengthy times of solitude provided adequate space for deep formation that needed done in my heart. At pivotal points in my vocational direction, relationships, and even schooling, I've encountered God on retreats. I'm convinced that we all need this time of retreat throughout our lives, but it is especially important for disciples early in their walk. A retreat is also important for those who have been walking with the Lord for a while, especially if they have not yet experienced this practice. When we make space for this, no matter our season of life or place along our journey, we allow God sufficient room to do some deep cleaning, healing, and renovating in our hearts. Certain spiritual work can only be done in solitude.

Let's remember that our need for solitude never goes away in our journey with God. Even the night before Jesus died, nearing the pinnacle of his earthly ministry, he made time to get away and pray to the Father in the Garden of Gethsemane. Even though his closest friends were just a stone's throw away, Jesus—"going a little farther"—went to be alone with God the Father (Matt. 26:39). Jesus' way of being alone emphasizes that the goal of solitude is not simply to be by ourselves, but to be alone *with God*. That's why Jesus said to his disciples, anticipating their desertion of him, "You will be scattered, each to his own home. You will leave me all alone. Yet I am not alone, for my Father is with me" (John 16:32). Jesus knew well the difference between solitude and isolation.

By practicing regular solitude, we allow God to train us to be alone with him, so that even when it's not our choice to be alone, we can connect with God in the lonely moments and seasons of life. Since our need for solitude remains constant throughout our lives, learning early and often how to connect with God through this discipline is helpful. We need the regular, short periods of solitude, along with the lengthier periods.

Supplemental Reading

In Dietrich Bonhoeffer's book *Life Together*, he offers insight into the importance of solitude in our lives together as Christians (see especially Chapter 3, "The Day Alone"). This book was originally written in 1939 in German and first published in English in 1954.

Your Spiritual Formation Plan

Take this opportunity to plan out your next steps with solitude.

What specific time and place will you practice daily or weekly solitude? How exactly do you want to use this time to connect with God?

_____
_____
_____
_____
_____
_____
_____
_____

What will be your specific time and place for an annual retreat? What's your plan for this getaway? Put something on the calendar, and go ahead and book it now.

_____
_____
_____
_____
_____
_____
_____
_____
_____

8

SILENCE

In this chapter you will:
- ☐ Make your plan for seeking silence.
- ☐ Ask for accountability to help you keep your plan for silence.

Silence is the necessary companion of solitude. When we experience both solitude and silence at the same time, we can most easily hear from God. Without silence, solitude loses its impact. Practicing silence means quieting human voices, physical distractions, and our own thoughts.

> We seek silence because our hearts long for quiet in a noisy world.

Thinking about "noise" in both literal and metaphorical terms is important. Our inner dialogue, for example, isn't audible sound, but it can actually be the loudest noise in our heads. So learning to be silent includes gaining the skills, with God's help, of quieting our thoughts. Inner noise can be unwanted thoughts. Most people have a message playing in their head that continually speaks to them about themselves. When this message is negative, it might speak a message about shame and guilt: "You're not worthy," or "You always do that." Whatever it is, the message is distracting and needs to be diminished.

Some messages can be less intense but still distracting. They might be about a to-do list, a deadline at work, or a project around the house. Noise can even come from unresolved tension in a relationship. Finding silence means placing those thoughts where they belong, not pushing them out by force. It often means submitting them to God by presenting "your requests to God" in prayer (Phil. 4:6). Ordering our thought-world through prayer helps us clear headspace to hear God's heart.

> God doesn't silence our thoughts by ignoring them;
> he quiets our minds by addressing them.

Silence is the spiritual discipline in which we let God's voice consume all invading voices. God doesn't think our thoughts for us, but he affects our thoughts within us. This happens as we seek God by the power of the Holy Spirit.

Then, we still face physical distractions and literal noises. Hearing a baby cry or a spouse in the other room or a lawn mower running outside—all of these noises distract us from seeking God in solitude. This discipline can be more difficult during certain seasons of life, which might mean we need to get creative. We might need to ask for extra help when we have a baby, for example, who requires constant attention. With help, we can find quiet in almost any life circumstance. Seeking silence means getting away from all types of noise, and as we grow in this practice, we learn our unique needs for clearing out distractions.

Solitude helps, but once we're alone, silence requires additional effort. That's why it's good to silence digital devices, turn off screens, and even turn off music to find peace and quiet. Whatever fills space in our hearts and makes it difficult to connect with God—however small it might be—can function as "noise."

God tells us in Scripture, "Be still, and know that I am God" (Ps. 46:10). This passage tells us that silence helps us to know God. The word for "be still" in Hebrew has to do with leaving or retreating, and it brings together solitude and silence in one word: *stillness*. Stillness affords us the opportunity to know God better by personally encountering God. While finding solitude and silence in today's world can be difficult, every ounce of effort we exert to find them is totally worth it!

Consider the role of silence and solitude in the prophet Samuel's life. When he was young, he first learned to hear God's voice in the quiet of the night when he was all alone (1 Sam. 3:1–11). Hearing clearly from God became increasingly important as Samuel grew up. When he was older, God asked him to choose the first two kings of Israel. Since he had learned to discern God's voice at a young age, he knew how to hear it when God asked him to choose Saul as Israel's first king: "This is the man I spoke to you about; he will govern my people" (1 Sam. 9:17). Then, when David appeared as the incumbent king, Samuel heard God say, "Rise and anoint him; he is the one" (1 Sam. 16:12). We have no evidence that God's voice in these cases was audible for Samuel. His voice was clearly discernable, though, whether it was audibly spoken or spoken only to his spirit. Whatever the case, Samuel learned how to hear God, which he first learned in solitude and silence.

The disciplines are never an end in themselves; they train us toward a greater good. As we grow in the discipline of silence, we too can learn to hear God's "still small voice," not only in quiet moments but also amid noise (1 Kgs. 19:12, KJV).

> ### Supplemental Reading
>
> Thomas R. Kelly's short book *A Testament of Devotion* offers a concise and delightful resource about living with simplicity and silence. Originally published in 1941, I recommend the 1996 reprint by HarperCollins Publishers, which includes an introduction by Richard J. Foster. See especially the last chapter, "The Simplification of Life."
>
> Another resource for learning to be alone with God is Brother Lawrence's *The Practice of the Presence of God*. He wrote it in the 1600s in French, but English versions today capture well the essence of his message about constant communication with God.

Your Spiritual Formation Plan

Use the space below to take your next steps toward finding silence.

What noises currently distract you? Consider noises in your life right now—both the obvious and subtle ones—that make silence difficult. Make a list here.

_____   _____
_____   _____
_____   _____
_____   _____
_____   _____
_____   _____
_____   _____
_____   _____

What is your plan for seeking silence from these noises during your times of solitude (and beyond)? What actions do you need to take in order to find silence from them?

_____
_____
_____
_____
_____
_____
_____
_____

Silence

What sort of accountability do you need for your next steps of pursuing regular silence? Who might be willing to offer this encouragement for you? Are you willing to ask them for help? If yes, then go ahead and ask them today.

_____
_____
_____
_____
_____
_____
_____

How will you know if you succeed in finding silence?

_____
_____
_____
_____
_____
_____
_____
_____
_____
_____
_____
_____
_____
_____
_____
_____

9

REST

> In this chapter you will:
> - ☐ Decide on a specific time frame for rest each week.
> - ☐ Make plans to say no to regular work.
> - ☐ Make plans for saying yes to connecting with God.

Throughout history the people of God have made a habit of finding rest, from the early days of Hebrew history until now. In recent history, though, our habits of rest seem to have changed. We've experienced an increase in mobility and technological advancements in our culture, yet have not used these advancements to find more rest. Instead, we've used them to busy ourselves with more things! Few people, in my observation, maintain a clearly defined time to rest each week that's grounded in a robust theology of rest. We implement notions of a "day off," or "taking time to be with the family," which have their place, but do these align with God's heart about rest? What does Scripture say about rest?

While other resources provide the necessary content for a robust theology of rest, this chapter can prime the pump for you. I have a specific outcome for you in this chapter. While it's not commonly practiced, implementing this could change your life:

> Set aside an entire, continuous twenty-four-hour period each week to rest by ceasing regular work so you can connect with God through prayer, his Word, and his people.

This specific suggestion is for those who want to pursue wholeness in their lives. Let me be clear: there's no law or requirement in Scripture to practice rest in exactly this way. Plus, there are vocations which make this not possible. But for most people, setting aside an entire day for this type of rest can work. It brings vitality to us as individuals, to our families, and to our churches. My recommendation comes from God's heart as seen in Scripture, along with precedents throughout faith history and my own experiences.

God's people often call this day of rest "Sabbath." Christians need not use that name to describe their day of rest, since "Sabbath" is a transliteration of the Hebrew word for Saturday. We can call it Sabbath, a Christian Sabbath, the Lord's Day, or some other name—the title isn't important. What we do with the Sabbath is what matters. God designed this day of rest to restore our souls in a unique way.

The new covenant ushered in by Jesus changed our understanding of rest, but it did not do away with the practice altogether. We know from Scripture that rest has always been important to God and still is important to God: God rested from his work on the seventh day of creation (Exod. 31:14–17); God anchored Sabbath rest for the Hebrews in their redemption from slavery in Egypt (Deut. 5:12–15); and "there remains . . . a Sabbath-rest for the people of God" (Heb. 4:9). These passages let us know there's something bigger to rest than mere ritualistic practice. Rest is near the very heart of God. That's why it's one of the Ten Commandments! When he gave us the new covenant in Christ, God's heart about rest did not change, but the specific way we understand it did change. Jesus came to fulfill the law, not abolish it (Matt. 5:17). So the question is not whether to rest but what rest looks like for disciples of Jesus.

Jesus fulfilled the meaning of the Sabbath rest for Christians, liberating us from any legalistic practice of it. He rebuked the Pharisees by saying, "The Sabbath was made for man, not man for the Sabbath" (Mark 2:27). Notice that Jesus *did not* do away with the Sabbath here. Jesus' disciples had unlawfully plucked heads of grain and eaten them on the Sabbath (v. 23). As a result, the Pharisees accused Jesus' disciples of breaking "the law." But Jesus outwitted them by citing three Old Testament passages and ended his argument with the words, "The Son of Man is Lord even of the Sabbath" (v. 28; see also Matt. 12:1–8). In the Gospels, not once did Jesus deny Sabbath-keeping; instead, he reoriented his audience toward the true meaning of the Sabbath.

Jesus' final words about lordship over the Sabbath include his authority over the very meaning of Sabbath rest. As the story unfolds—we learn an important truth:

> The Sabbath is not just about rest but also about restoration.

We see this play out as the story continues. Jesus effectively claimed dominion over the Sabbath and clarified its meaning in one fell swoop. He did this as he transitioned from a debate-style discussion into real-life action. He walked from the grainfields to the synagogue, where he healed a man whose hand was shriveled. Through this healing, Jesus made the same point, but now through his actions: Sabbath is a day for restoration, not quibbling over technicalities. So Jesus affirmed Sabbath rest and at the same time redefined it—but he never did away with it.

Nowhere in the remainder of the New Testament is the Sabbath rejected either. In fact if anything, the New Testament writers reinforce Jesus' teaching on this. The only negative command about Sabbath in the New Testament comes from Paul, who issues a clear warning about not judging anyone on how they observe Sabbath rest (Col. 2:13–17). Importantly, he does not say, *Do not practice the Sabbath anymore.* There's a major difference between redefining the Sabbath and rejecting the day altogether. Most of us treat the Sabbath as though it were abolished, yet we're seeing that Scripture does not reject but instead redefines this day of rest. I suggest, therefore, that we ought to live true to the impetus to rest, as Jesus defined it.

Church history reveals how Christians have continued the tradition of setting aside an entire day of rest each week. Very early in our history, Christians changed their day of worship from Saturday to Sunday because Jesus was resurrected on a Sunday. Since that time, Christians throughout history have gathered together on Sundays to celebrate our redemption.

Many people today consider going to church on Sunday their "Sabbath" practice, which is great! But there's more to it than showing up to church. The issue is that few people think clearly about the purpose of that day—and what to do during their day of rest.

We need to set clear boundaries for ourselves, and incorporate certain spiritual practices for our day of rest. That's why you have space in this workbook to create a clear, well-defined plan for yourself. Remember that we have immense freedom to practice and plan our day of rest as we see fit. We have no certain laws to obey, only God's heart to pursue. In order to do that, setting aside one day a week for resting in the Lord is important. Why? Because God rested, God's people have rested throughout history, and resting can be a life-giving practice for us too.

> Sabbath is a gift from God to be received, not a law to be followed.

In summary, we don't simply stop working on this day of rest; we stop working *in order to connect with God*. What exactly do we do on this day of rest then?

I recommend a two-step framework for cultivating a habit of rest in your life: the first step is to *stop working*, and the second step is to *engage with God*. These steps work together like the steps of a dance because we cannot adequately engage God with other believers if we're all at work! We need to sync up by having a common day of rest with those in our close fellowship, when possible. We find this principle of both stopping and engaging embedded in the Bible, when God said, "Tomorrow is to be a day of rest, a holy Sabbath to the LORD" (Exod. 16:23). The Sabbath is to be "holy"—set apart from the other days of the week—but also directional, not static. Our rest is holy *to the Lord*. We don't disappear on the couch on Sabbath, or binge on media, or just do nothing. We embrace the orientation, direction, and purpose of Sabbath by resting *to God*.

Here's what this can look like: *Step 1: Say no to regular work.* Decide on a particular day each week to stop working. Request off work, communicate with your family about the details of the day, and make plans with other believers. Set boundaries around this time, and while you can remain flexible, don't make a habit of bending your boundaries. Make it possible not to check email, for example, and take care of yardwork on a different day. Complete tasks such as preparing food beforehand, if possible, so you can focus your attention directly on God.

Step 2: Say yes to connecting with God through prayer, his Word, and his people. This is the positive side of what you do while you're not working on this day. Focus your engagement with God during your day of rest on three activities with God's people: 1) praying together, 2) reading God's Word together, and 3) gathering together. Sit down with your family and a group from your church to read Scripture—even long portions at a time. Spend time praying with one another. And simply rest together. Some of the best God-centered discussions happen when you simply hang out with God's people. Remember to make this day fun and something you look forward to! *One note to young families: you need to consider how to integrate your kids graciously into this, so feel free to experiment and find out what works for your family in particular—and keep experimenting as your kids grow up.*

Supplemental Reading

Mark Buchanan's book *The Rest of God: Restoring Your Soul by Restoring Sabbath* (Nashville: Thomas Nelson, 2006) offers a rich case for restoring Sabbath practices. I highly recommend this resource because it was the book that convinced me years ago to restore the Sabbath in my life. I want to also mention my class session on rest in my *Spiritual Formation* video course, which you can access at himpublications.com/spiritual. This class session contains a fuller version of my biblical theology of rest.

Your Spiritual Formation Plan

Now it's time to make your plan for rest! Use the space below to take your next steps.

When will you regularly "rest to God"? Name a specific day of the week and write out a precise time frame each week your day of rest will begin and end.

_____

_____

_____

What do you need to say no to in order to make this day different from every other day of the week?

_____	_____
_____	_____
_____	_____
_____	_____

What do you need to say yes to in order to connect with God meaningfully through prayer, his Word, and his people? Use this space to make plans for regularly gathering with God's people on this day.

_____

_____

_____

_____

_____

_____

_____

_____

10

READING SCRIPTURE

> In this chapter you will:
> ☐ Understand the ABCs of Scripture reading.
> ☐ Select a book for your book study.
> ☐ Pick at least one passage for concentrated reading.

Reading Scripture pairs well with the disciplines we've covered so far—silence, solitude, and even rest—which is why I covered those disciplines first. In this chapter, I describe three core practices of reading Scripture for individuals. I call them the "ABCs" of Scripture reading: *All the Bible, Book Study,* and *Concentrated Reading*. Each one serves a unique role in your formation process. My goal here is to introduce these three practices and help you navigate the basics for each one.

Before we get into the details, though, we must remember an important truth that helps keep our interpretations of the Bible in check:

> God gave Scripture to the church, not just to individuals.

This means that while we can read and study on our own, we should never read Scripture *in isolation*. Even when reading alone, we remember what we learned from others in the church, and we must always submit our understanding to correction that can come from those around us, those over us, and those who've come before us. By submitting our understanding to reliable handlers of the Word, we're saying, "I'm not my own final authority on the meaning of God's Word!" We allow these reliable teachers—especially those God has placed over us and whom we personally know—to guide us along the way, as we open ourselves to possible instruction, correction, and even challenges. We must read Scripture in fellowship with believers because only then can we reliably study on our own. So assuming we're reading Scripture with others, individual study can be immensely fruitful.

As you study on your own, the goal is to cultivate a vibrant and joyful Scripture-reading life. I've identified three vital mile markers as signposts along the way toward that goal. You will see them throughout your journey because they appear in different ways as you progress, and like the ABCs of English, you never graduate from them. So take the necessary time to learn them now. They are listed below in order of priority. Do them in sequential order at first, but as you grow in reading Scripture, you'll find that they overlap and work together in synchronicity.

All the Bible. The first step of intentionally reading Scripture is to read all of the Bible. *"All scripture* is inspired by God and is useful for teaching, for reproof, for correction, and for training in righteousness, so that everyone who belongs to God may be proficient, equipped for every good work" (2 Tim. 3:16–17, NRSV). God inspired all of Scripture, so we must read all of it! This is the first mile marker of cultivating a vibrant Scripture-reading life. It's first because it allows you to better grasp the parts of the Bible by seeing the whole.

While we need to continue reading the entirety of Scripture throughout our lives, the first read-through is vital. I often wonder for Christians who never read the whole Bible, *What if God provided the key to a breakthrough in your life in a part of the Bible you've never read, and you simply need to read it?* Let me pose a similar question to you: If you found out today that God had inspired sixty-*seven* books of the Bible, instead of just sixty-*six*, would you read the missing book right away? Of course, that's not true because the canon of Scripture is closed. But that's how Christians should treat any part of the Bible they've never read—like the treasure it is! Perhaps God has a special word for you from his fixed Word, if only you will read the book of his special revelation. So start by reading all the Bible. If you've read parts here and there, go ahead and read it all, cover to cover.

Book Study. The second mile marker is completing a book study. A book study is systematically studying a single book in the Bible. Choose one of the sixty-six books of the Bible and go deep into it. You can complete a simple or a detailed book study. A simple book study goes something like this: 1) read the book once to get the big picture, 2) read the book again and write down themes from the book, and then 3) read the book a third time to decide the main theme. That's the simple book study.

A detailed book study is an activity of the Inductive Bible Study method. *Inductive* means that you make conclusions by compiling clues as you go along. The opposite is *deductive,* which means starting with a conclusion, and

Reading Scripture

then unpacking its meaning and logic along the way. The Inductive Bible Study method involves systematically studying one book of the Bible as you analyze the context to determine the meaning of specific passages within it. See Appendix B of this workbook for step-by-step instructions for completing a detailed book study using this method.

My goal for you in this chapter is to help you pick one book of the Bible to be your companion during this season of your journey with God. This goal works with both types of book studies (simple and detailed). That means you need to select a book of the Bible! This is exciting because you get to choose what you want to study.

As I mentioned about desire in general, being honest with yourself about your desire for Scripture reading is important. Below you'll answer a question, "Which book of the Bible do you want to study?" When you answer this question, it's not about what you *should* study but what you *want* to study. Think and pray through it, until you're clear-minded before the Lord about which book to choose. If you get stuck, ask for help, and try to select the book on your own, not letting someone else pick this for you. It's like picking a friend for a journey. When you choose a book of the Bible as your traveling companion, you'll be glad you willingly chose how to spend your time in the coming weeks and months.

How does God work in this selection process? He guides us as we take action. So ask God for direction to start, then pay attention to what book grabs your attention. Trust that God is at work in your heart and mind. Most of the time, when I'm operating from a healthy place spiritually, the Holy Spirit guides my attraction toward a certain biblical book. I don't worry too much about whether "God told me" to read a certain book; I rest in the fact that it's all God's Word anyway! His Word still speaks because it's living and active (Heb. 4:12). So there's no risk of choosing the "wrong" book to read. But once a decision is made, commit to it for a season.

Stay in that one book for three to nine months at a time as a rule of thumb. Based on my experience and the wisdom of others, Christians need at least three months of regular reading to let a particular book's message saturate their hearts.

Concentrated Reading. The third mile maker of deep Scripture reading is concentrated reading. This is focusing your thoughts on a single verse, phrase, or word from Scripture. This takes the form of two skill sets: meditation and memorization. I listed concentrated reading third because while you can do it at any point of your journey with any passage, it's most effective when you've passed mile marker one and two already. By reading the whole Bible and understanding the overall picture of a particular book of the Bible, you can meditate on a specific verse from that book and mine rich raw materials. When you're getting your feet wet in Scripture reading, meditate on a passage from the book you're studying. But as you progress, remember that the process is not always linear. Sometimes you'll focus on a verse from a book you haven't studied in depth, like a verse from the Psalms, as an example. That's good too.

Meditate on a Scripture passage before memorizing it because meditating helps you memorize, but memorizing doesn't necessarily help you meditate. Meditating on Scripture means picking one verse in the Bible and dwelling on it before the Lord.

> Meditating on Scripture is more about heart-level reading than mind-level analysis.

Psalm 1:2 says that the person who "meditates day and night" on the Word is blessed. Unlike any other practice, from my experience, meditation helps us move Scripture from our heads to our hearts.

As we allow God's Word to saturate our hearts through meditation, we will find ourselves memorizing Scripture. Rote memorization is valuable, but if it doesn't lead to delightful meditation on the Word, our priorities are disordered. Find what works for you. Whatever way you come at it, remember that memorization exists for the purpose of meditation. We memorize to help us meditate when we don't have the Bible in front of us. No matter our age, we can all memorize Scripture. With God's strength, you can do this! See Appendix C for some key Scripture verses for meditation and memorization. Those are the three mile markers—the ABCs of Scripture reading!

I provided this high-level vision for forming your Scripture reading plan because starting on the right foot is important. So what's your next step? If you haven't read the entire Bible, start there. Maybe you've read the New Testament but not the Old. Go ahead and read the Old! Spend the time you need to read the whole Bible in a period of three months, six months, or a year—whatever time frame works for your current season of life. Once you've done that, complete a book study. Then, as you spend time with that book, practice meditating on and memorizing Scripture from it.

If you feel overwhelmed with any of this, take heart! God energizes us as we cooperate with him. And remember, the disciplines work together, so use your plans for silence, solitude, and rest to read Scripture. Your weekly day of

Reading Scripture

rest and your annual retreat can also provide time to go deep into Scripture reading.

> ### Supplemental Reading
>
> Michael Casey's book *Sacred Reading: The Ancient Art of Lectio Divina* (Liguori, MO: Liguori Publications, 1996) is a rich resource for going deeper into concentrated reading of Scripture. As a Cistercian monk, Casey applies what he's learned from ancient monastic traditions to modern readers of all types today. I recommend this book, but a fair warning: it goes deep!

All the Bible. Have you read the entire Bible? If not, what's your plan for doing so?

Book Study. If you've read the whole Bible, which book of the Bible do you want to study as your companion for this season of your journey? Do you want to do the simple version described above or the detailed version (see Appendix B for more information)? If it's your first time, go with the simple version for starters. That way you can keep moving along! Then, for your next season, try the more complex version. Whether you're doing the simple or detailed version, what's your plan for finishing it?

Concentrated Reading. As you get into your book study, which passage do you want to use to meditate on and memorize? If you want to pick a passage from elsewhere in the Bible, see Appendix C for ideas. Are you willing to commit to doing this within a certain time frame? If so, write a date next to each passage for when you'll focus your concentrated reading on it.

11

PRAYER

In this chapter you will:
- ☐ Decide on a type of prayer list to start.
- ☐ Write your prayer list.

Scripture is God's first word to us in prayer. That's why prayer comes after Scripture reading in this workbook. When we read Scripture, we're listening to God's heart. And as we listen to God's heart, we're moved to pray. When we're not feeling particularly spiritual, though, it can be hard to pray. Simply reading Scripture can help us start to pray.

God gives us prayer as a primary way of connecting with him, but many people face the challenge of making the time to pray. Once we make the time, the challenge then becomes filling that time with heartfelt and meaningful prayers. Why can prayer feel like such a challenge? One reason people struggle in their prayer lives is because they pray haphazardly or at random. My prayers have been like that too at times. When we don't have a thoughtful prayer life, we might squeeze a prayer in before bed or at a meal, but deep down, we know God offers more. God wants to give us a vibrant connection with him through prayer. The simplest, most practical remedy for haphazard praying is keeping a prayer list, and this chapter helps you create one.

As you journey deeper into the heart of God, a prayer list helps you structure your prayer life. It encourages you to be specific and diligent in prayer.

> A prayer list frees you up by reigning you in.

In no way does it limit your prayer life; instead, a prayer list increases your memory to pray for what's important to you! You will have an opportunity to start a prayer list at the end of this chapter, and as you do, remember this: keeping a prayer list helps you keep track of what's close to your heart and what's close to God's heart during a particular season of life.

Jesus gave us the framework for prayer with the Our Father Prayer (also known as the Lord's Prayer) from Matthew 6:9–13, but we still fill it with our own unique prayers. That's where the prayer list comes in. Combining your own prayer list with Jesus' framework brings together the best of both worlds: praying with both structure and spontaneity. I'll explain more on how to create a list, but first I want to address a common barrier some people run into when starting their list.

Some Christians who consider creating a prayer list feel hesitant about making their prayer life feel forced. They wonder, *Isn't keeping a prayer list legalistic?* Let me address that question: while it's possible to lose the heart behind this practice and turn prayer into a new law for yourself, structuring your prayer life doesn't have to lead to obligation in your prayer life. Sometimes praying involves a sense of duty, but with God duty can turn into delight. Plus, God can help you maintain a pure heart even while you order your prayer life with a prayer list.

> A prayer list is a tool that helps you organize your prayers, not an obligation you must follow.

It can help us pray more often and more fruitfully. It helps us put the most important items of our hearts on the table of our communion with God, front and center. Consider this exercise your invitation to organize your prayer life in a way that suits your personality and style.

Start with one of two basic options: a bullet-point prayer list or a days-of-the-week prayer list. You can use the space on the page at the end of this chapter to start your list, but feel free to start a list on a separate sheet of paper and adapt my suggestions to create an entirely different kind prayer list that best suits you. I'll describe the two basic options and let you decide.

Bullet-point prayer list. The simplest prayer list is a bullet-point prayer list of the people, events, and issues on your heart. Under "Prayer List" at the top write the date you start the list. This helps you chronicle God's answers to your prayers. When you create new lists in the future, you can use a page from your journal, a sheet of loose-leaf paper, or a note-keeping app on your digital device. Whatever you use, make sure it's easily accessible at your time of regular prayer. As you prayerfully form your list, write what comes to mind. Create your entire list in one or two sittings, praying as you go. One more tip: leave space next to each bullet to add notes and answers to your prayers in the coming months.

Days-of-the-week prayer list. A second type of prayer list is categorized by the days of the week. This style works best for those who intend to set aside daily time to pray but who also want to pray for some items only once a week. For example, you might want to pray for your immediate family members every day but for people at work only once a week. There's no shame in praying for someone or something just once a week—that's better than not praying for them at all! When you create this list, try to come up with daily prayer items in one sitting, and then over the course of a week, as you pray, jot down what you want to pray for each day of the week. Your list helps you to focus each day's prayers so you can cover more ground more consistently. I included at the end of this chapter prayer ideas for each day of the week to get your wheels spinning.

As you decide how to structure your prayer list, consider what's on your heart during this season of life. Remember, you can always adapt your prayer list. You can even write your prayer list in pencil if you want to easily change it. Use all these suggestions or adapt them to come up with your own style. Maybe you will combine my suggestions with another model, or try something entirely different altogether. You might, for example, use the way Jesus prays in John 17 as a model for how to structure your prayers: he prayed for himself first (vv. 1–5), then his closest friends (vv. 6–19), and finally those on the perimeter of his influence (vv. 20–23). There's no single way to take the next step as you bring order to your prayer life.

Start a fresh list every two to six months, as a rule of thumb. That time frame comes from my experience, because typically when I use the same prayer list for longer than six months, it starts to feel stale and I know it's time to start a new prayer list. I usually carry over some items from my old list to my new list, but sometimes I start from scratch. Why does keeping a fresh list matter? It can serve as a chronicle of God's work in our lives as he answers our prayers. This helps to grow our trust in him over time by looking back at what God has done and is still doing in our lives.

In this chapter's exercise, write down what type of prayer list you plan to use, then go ahead and start filling in your list! Fill your list with what you want to pray for during this season of your life. If you're feeling stagnant in prayer, your list will help you get into the habit of regularly—even systematically—praying for what is most important to you. We make lists for so many other areas of our lives, so why not for our prayers? Consider this initial list simply as your next step in prayer. Once you've gotten into the habit of using a prayer list, you will better know how to adapt the practice to suit your personality and preferences.

If you decide to go with the days-of-the-week list, consider a few examples for what to pray on each day of the week, then make your list. These ideas should help you get going:

- DAILY PRAYER: Pray for yourself, your immediate family members, those discipling you, those you're discipling, and important vocational pursuits.
- SUNDAY: Pray for your church and the elders and deacons at your church by name.
- MONDAY: Pray for extended family members by name.
- TUESDAY: Pray for members of your discipleship group(s) by name.
- WEDNESDAY: Pray for coworkers, clients, and others at work by name.
- THURSDAY: Pray for the lost by name.
- FRIDAY: Pray for missionaries by name.
- SATURDAY: Pray for your neighbors by name.

Supplemental Reading

Jim Cymbala's book *Fresh Wind, Fresh Fire: What Happens When God's Spirit Invades the Hearts of His People* (Grand Rapids: Zondervan, 2018) is an inspiring story about the life-changing power of prayer. This book chronicles the story of how praying every Sunday before church service brought revival in and through the Brooklyn Tabernacle. It was originally published in 1997.

PRAYER LIST

Start Date: _____

12

FASTING

In this chapter you will:
- ☐ Start your next fast.
- ☐ Make a plan for regular fasting.
- ☐ Ask someone to fast regularly with you.

Fasting from food serves as an extension of prayer, and it uniquely helps us connect with God. While we can pray using different postures, fasting involves our bodies in its own way. Fasting should be combined with actual spoken prayers, but in a sense, fasting itself is a prayer—a prayer that we speak to God with our whole bodies.

Going without food is a rather strange means of God's grace, isn't it? It's not too often that we consider hunger pangs a gift! Furthermore, the apostle Paul affirms food as a good thing when he says to Timothy about abstaining from certain foods, "For everything God created is good, and nothing is to be rejected if it is received with thanksgiving" (1 Tim. 4:4). So if food was created by God to be enjoyed, then why should we abstain from it?

We can safely say that fasting is a Christian discipline because not only did Jesus fast but he also told us how to fast (Matt. 6:16–18). Let me be clear that no command in the New Testament says *Christians must fast*, but the expectation remains. Plus, the experience of Christians through the millennia proves that this practice holds an important place in the spiritual disciplines for disciples of Jesus. What adds to its importance is how it can intensify other disciplines, such as prayer, reading Scripture, solitude, confession, and listening. Here is an important truth to remember:

> Fasting is a gift from God.

When words do not give enough voice to our prayers, fasting utilizes our very bodies to help us pray with every fiber of our beings. This is a gift, without which we would be limited in the depth of our abilities to express desperation to God.

How does this fit within the spiritual formation journey? Through fasting we mysteriously connect with God through self-denial, and God forms our souls to follow Jesus with increased levels of self-denial. All this gives us reason to fast, but how do we fast on a practical level? Let me explain the purpose of fasting, as I understand it, then offer some suggestions for how to plan your fasting habits.

We can pray and fast on all sorts of occasions, but one basic longing drives all types of fasting. It's a common thread that ties all examples of fasting in the Bible together: *desperation* (for example, Deut. 9:9; 2 Sam. 12:15–17; Est. 4:1; 1 Kgs. 19:8; Neh. 9:1–3; Dan. 9:1–5; Jon. 3:5; Matt. 4:1–11; Acts 9:9; 13:2–3). People who fasted in biblical history were all *desperate for something*. Whether desperate for salvation, restoration, or renewal, fasting was the means through which God's people expressed their desperation. Sometimes we fast to repent over our sin or selfishness; sometimes we fast about an important event or situation; and sometimes we fast because we're sorrowful or sad. Whatever our reason, fasting gives voice to our prayers of desperation like nothing else.

We fast alone and with others. When we fast with others, we experience a certain kind of *power*, so I encourage leaders to initiate fasting with their church, group, or family. And when we fast together, we can encourage each other in this discipline because let's face it: going without food is challenging! Plus, when we fast as a group, we can learn from others how to do it. In the Old Testament and in the New Testament, we find records of God's people fasting together, so we have a strong biblical precedent for group fasts. But what does a group fast look like today? A church can fast every week on a certain day of the week or a certain month of the year, and other fasts might come in response to a specific circumstance or situation in the group.

While these types of group fasts carry immense value—whether it's with your family, your small group, your entire church, or even your city—the main point of this chapter is about helping you as an individual take your next steps in fasting. Even so, ask a friend or a mentor to join you as you grow! And if you're a leader, don't wait until you've figured it all out before you invite others to join you. You can all learn together.

As you learn to fast, remember the immense freedom, grace, and mercy you have in Christ. Fasting from food presents a unique challenge because it's so bodily and visceral, which can cause us to forget the basics. I've personally experienced and seen in others acute temptations with regard to feeling guilt, shame, and comparison as they begin this practice. That's why, I suppose, we don't find specific regulations about the particulars of fasting in the Bible, and why we find heart-level instructions in places such as Isaiah 58:3–9; Zechariah 7:1–7; and Matthew 6:16–18.

My suggestion, then, is to grow in this discipline incrementally. That is, don't bite off more than you can chew! As you start small and go slow, invite people to fast with you, even if you're not yet able to guide anyone on how to fast. If this practice is new to you, you might want to start by eliminating snacks or one small meal for one day. Then, go without one regular meal; after that, try going without food for two meals. After that, go thirty-six hours without food, then three days, and so on. These are common increments of progression in fasting, but there's no set formula or path. And everyone who's new to fasting should consider consulting their doctor first, especially as you consider fasting for longer periods of time.

As you cultivate habits of personal fasting, make space for both spontaneous and regular fasting. *Spontaneous fasting* can happen when we feel a special desire to fast. Fasting when we have an acute sense of desperation tunes us into our spiritual desire for connecting with God through this discipline. By cultivating our relationship with God on this spontaneous level, we can more naturally plunge into regular fasting, when we don't particularly feel like it.

If you want to start fasting but the moment of decision is not "coming to you," try a spontaneous fast. Here's one way you can start, and it works especially well if you've never fasted and you want to make sure to engage your heart: Put this chapter of the workbook in front of you every night before bed for the next seven days. Use that as a practical reminder to gauge your heart's readiness. Each night ask yourself, *Do I feel desperate for God about anything? Is there anything weighing heavily on my heart? Is there something in my life that feels like a spiritual burden?* Even ask, *What is going on in my life that is heavy on your heart, God?* Allow God's heart to affect your heart through these questions. This type of self-reflective prayer can help you measure your level of desperation. When you feel desperate for something, just go for it the next day! That'll be your next spontaneous fast.

You don't have to feel "super spiritual" to start, or even hear directly from God about when to fast. Withhold judgment about when you decide to fast, especially when you're starting out. Decide on a day for fasting, then make preparations and adjust your schedule as best you can. Even though this is spontaneous, make sure to prepare yourself spiritually for the fast by praying ahead of time and thinking about your purpose for the fast. And remember to communicate well with those who will be impacted by your fast.

Regular fasting. As you grow in this discipline, you will likely experience a desire for more regular fasting by a growing sense of desperation before God. We become more sensitive to what breaks God's heart through fasting, and we grow in our knowledge of God and of ourselves through this discipline as well. So as your sense of general desperation for God grows, regular fasting becomes the planned way for making space to express your desperation to God.

Most people who regularly fast, pick a day once or twice a week to fast. You may have heard that the Pharisees fasted on Mondays and Thursdays, but did you know that some of the earliest Christians fasted twice a week as well, on Wednesdays and Fridays? They did this not because they were legalists but because they so valued this practice that they made regular plans for it. There's no general legislation with regard to fasting, though, so receive the freedom to practice this as you see fit. And remember to be flexible! Knowing when to flex your plans due to an unexpected change of plans is an art. It's okay, even good, to be flexible, especially as you're getting your feet wet in the practice of fasting. In summary, as you begin to make plans, start with spontaneous fasting, then begin adding structure to your habits with regular fasting.

Supplemental Reading

Dave Clayton's book *Revival Starts Here: A Short Conversation on Prayer, Fasting, and Revival for Beginners Like Me* (Nashville: HIM Publications, 2018) provides a simple and inspiring introduction to prayer and fasting for revival. It's been used by hundreds of churches and tens of thousands of Christians to pray for awakening. It's practical, relatable, and challenging.

Fasting

Use the space below to take your next steps with fasting.

What is your past experience with fasting? Do you have any hesitations before you begin your next fast?

___

Spontaneous fasting. Are you ready to start fasting? If so, during what time frame do you want to start your next fast? Use the questions mentioned in this chapter (see the "spontaneous fasting" section above) to help you make a game-time decision.

_____
_____
_____

Regular fasting. When you're ready for regular fasting, on which day(s) do you want to fast? If you're not ready yet, what's stopping you from committing to regular fasting?

_____
_____
_____
_____
_____
_____
_____
_____
_____
_____
_____

Group fasting. With whom can you regularly fast? Consider asking a friend, family member, or your group to fast with you.

_____

13

SERVICE

> In this chapter you will:
> ☐ Identify a person or a group to serve.
> ☐ Make an initial plan for serving them.
> ☐ Ask someone to serve with you.

As I mentioned in the introduction of this workbook, the ultimate goal of spiritual formation is love: God uses the spiritual disciplines to pour out his grace into our hearts to make us more loving. Love is the highest virtue in the New Testament, but the second most-prized virtue is humility. So how do the disciplines cultivate humility in us? Certain disciplines effect humility in us more than others, and four disciplines in particular most directly impact our growth in humility: service, submission, confession, and listening. We'll cover each one in turn in the coming chapters, starting with service.

When we physically serve others, we reveal with our actions a humble heart. Expressing humility happens when we "go low" and serve. Service expresses humility, but it also cultivates humility in us. That's why service is a means of God's grace. It's beautiful:

> God forms us through service to become more like Christ.

Jesus served others during his earthly ministry by washing feet, and he calls us to serve one another in the same way: "As I have loved you, so you must love one another" (John 13:34). In John 13, service looks like washing the feet of our brothers and sisters in Christ. We serve the world, no doubt, but our first priority is to serve "one another" (see also Matt. 25:31–46). Service is first for those in the church, as we take care of our brothers and sisters in Christ, then for the world. Only a healthy and whole church can stoop low enough to serve the world with the humility of Christ.

Your Spiritual Formation Plan

In Matthew 25, Jesus describes six ways we can serve one another. More ways exist, but these six are important, even foundational, ways to serve those in our spiritual family. And when we serve others, we serve Christ himself. Jesus said, "Whatever you did for one of the least of these brothers of mine, you did for me" (Matt. 25:40). When we neglect to serve others, though, we reject Jesus himself: "Whatever you did not do for one of the least of these, you did not do for me" (Matt. 25:45). So the focus of Jesus' words in both Matthew 25 and in John 13 is the family of God first. But it's vital to remember that while the biblical call to serve begins with those in the church, it doesn't end with the church (Matt. 5:38–42; Eph. 6:7). We serve one another so that we can serve the world stronger together! It's worth repeating:

> Only a healthy and whole church can stoop low enough to serve the world with the humility of Christ.

In our call to service, it's important to remember our limitations. This means that while no particular one of us can do *everything* that needs to be done in the world, we can each do *something*.

So what can you do? And what are you willing to do to serve "the least of these" in the family of God and beyond? Pause to read Matthew 25:31–46 right now, and as you read, consider the six types of service Jesus mentions:

- Giving food to the hungry
- Giving drink to the thirsty
- Welcoming the stranger
- Clothing the naked
- Taking care of the sick
- Visiting the imprisoned

When you finish reading Matthew 25:31–46, pick up here.

As Jesus' words about service in Matthew 25 show, service is not a mere one-time event, service project, or "service day." Those can be good activities, but there's a more relational approach than one-time events tend to be. Healthy relationships require time, and we develop them through repeated touch-points. Serving is not a nine-to-five job that ends just before dinner.

> Serving is a way of life that characterizes everything we do.

Service

What does it mean to "serve others" exactly? It means we literally help others physically. It seems sort of funny, of all things, that Jesus asked us to wash one another's feet in John 13! But his command was intentional. He didn't issue a high and lofty command by saying, "Devote yourself to the mission by sailing the seven seas for my kingdom!" Foreign mission work that requires overseas travel is a great sacrifice and service for God, but that's not everyone's calling. When it comes to the essential and universal command for all disciples to serve, Jesus said something much more earthy: "Now that I, your Lord and Teacher, have washed your feet, you also should wash one another's feet" (John 13:14). Stinky-feet service keeps us grounded as we move forward on the humble journey of discipleship. Disciples of Jesus, no matter their positions, are never above service because they're never above their master, Jesus.

Serving others is also personal. Notice in Matthew 25:31–46 Jesus didn't say, "I was hungry and you wrote a check to the World Hunger Foundation," or "I was naked and you dropped clothes off at your local thrift store." He said, "I was hungry and *you* gave me something to eat," and "I needed clothes and *you* clothed me" (Matt. 25:35–36). Jesus asks us to serve personally. While I think contributing money and donating clothes to the poor has its place, there's something important about personally meeting the face of Christ in others as we serve face-to-face. We must remember that anyone can be in the kinds of poverty Jesus describes in Matthew 25 at any given moment, which means opportunities to serve exist all around us—if only we have the eyes to see it.

The aim of this chapter is to help you take your next step with regard to service. But before we move to action, I want to describe a few guardrails to help you avoid common service pitfalls. First, Christians sometimes think you need to have the spiritual "gift of service" in order to serve others, but this is simply not true. We serve others because Jesus served and because he commanded us to serve one another. Service is a lifestyle that characterizes disciples of Jesus, not a one-time event or a special-occasion discipline. It's a habit of the heart that permeates our entire lives.

Another potential pitfall is serving with the wrong motives. Sometimes, we're tempted to serve in order to gain approval from others. In this scenario, we want to please people in unhealthy ways. If the people we're serving are not happy with our work, we might get in a tizzy or caught up in their disappointment. This affects the quality and depth of our service. As a result, we serve only on a surface-level or to be seen by others. We must guard against this type of service, and we can! In Christ, we have power from God to "serve wholeheartedly, as if . . . serving the Lord" (Eph. 6:7). God can purify us and bring order to disordered motives in our hearts as we submit ourselves to him. We serve not in order to find our value or worth in the measure of our service but because we are servants of Christ.

Finally, we must guard against the messiah complex. When someone has a messiah complex with regard to service, that means they think their service can save the world. We recognize this in a few clearly discernable ways. Someone with a messiah complex always serves but doesn't easily receive service done for them. They work their fingers to the bone, but it's never enough; they always have to do more. This goes beyond a hard work ethic because they believe on some level *the salvation of the world depends on them*. We don't need to act like a savior, though, because One already offered salvation to the whole world. Those who carry this struggle forget that we sometimes need to receive acts of service and not be the one serving. We can't save the world, so we rest on Jesus' ultimate physical service for humanity, even as we take up the towel and basin to serve.

As you grow in service, start by focusing on just one of the six physical ways of serving from Matthew 25. Look at these six ways to serve and pray about where to find persons in need. If it's not immediately obvious, ask your church about needs that exist. Talk with a leader at your church to find out where others from your church already serve or who has a specific need. Find where God is already at work and join him there. Either way, go ahead and get started! Take your next step with excitement because when you physically serve your brothers and sisters, you can expect to meet Jesus in your service.

Supplemental Reading

Steve Corbett and Brian Fikkert's book *When Helping Hurts: How to Alleviate Poverty Without Hurting the Poor . . . and Yourself* (Chicago: Moody, 2009) is essential reading for anyone living in the West who want to engage the poor. This book goes deeper into important pitfalls that are common for Westerners today, and provides a helpful biblical framework for thinking about four different kinds of poverty.

Service

Use the space below to take your next steps with regard to service.

Whom can you consistently and personally serve over the next few months? Identify a single individual or group of people, even though your service may grow from there. You might want to prayerfully read again through Matthew 25:31–46, and ask God, "Where are you among the least of these in my life and in the world?"

Your Spiritual Formation Plan

How can you serve this person or group? Write out your thoughts and jot down your initial plan here.

_____
_____
_____
_____
_____
_____
_____
_____
_____
_____
_____
_____
_____
_____
_____
_____
_____
_____
_____
_____

Who might join you? Are you willing to ask them? If so, go ahead and ask them today!

_____
_____
_____

14

SUBMISSION

> In this chapter you will:
> ☐ Identify any areas of rebellion in your life.
> ☐ Make plans to change and become more submissive.

People generally don't enjoy being told to submit. Submission, though, is an important aspect of our journey, from the first step of following Jesus to the last. We committed to submitting ourselves totally to Jesus' leadership, his rulership, and his authority when we decided to follow him. Submission is the name of the game for disciples!

> Submission means willingly cooperating with those in positions of authority in our lives.

Yet many of us resist authority, making our discipleship journey difficult. When God prods us to stay on the straight and narrow path, our rebellious hearts "kick against the goads" (Acts 26:14). But God expects us to reject this rebellious posture: "Do not be like the horse or the mule, which have no understanding but must be controlled by bit and bridle or they will not come to you" (Ps. 32:9).

One way God makes us holy is through our acts of submission. Submitting to others forms us into humble persons. Like with service, submission has a way of bringing us low and forming us to be humble like Christ. We have the power and an example of what submission looks like in him. Jesus submitted himself to God, to his parents, and even to the governing authorities who put him to death on a cross (John 14:31; Luke 2:51; John 19:11). His life is our example of humble submission. Jesus did this all as the King of kings and Lord of lords, even when he was treated unjustly. But when he comes back at the Second Coming to judge the living and the dead, he will bring final justice on earth (Rev. 19:11–16). In the meantime, we follow him and humbly submit, as he did, under God's delegated authorities in this world.

God has placed seven types of authorities over us in different spheres of life (listed below). These are the main types of authority in Scripture to whom we are called to submit—God himself being at the top of the list. Each type holds a certain amount of authority in our lives, and that authority comes from God. That's what God's "delegated authority" means: he has distributed his authority to certain positions of power on earth.

I inserted only a short quote from each passage below to give you a sense for each one. Read each verse in context for a fuller understanding of biblical submission and authority. This is a good starting point, though, for understanding our general call to submission. God calls us to submit to these seven authorities:

1. God himself	"Submit yourselves, then, to God." — James 4:7
2. Church leaders	"Obey your leaders and submit to their authority." — Hebrews 13:17
3. Believers in general	"Submit to one another out of reverence for Christ." — Ephesians 5:21
4. Spouse	"Wives, submit to your husbands as to the Lord. . . . Husbands, love your wives, just as Christ loved the church and gave himself up for her." — Ephesians 5:22, 25
5. Parents	"Children, obey your parents in the Lord, for this is right." — Ephesians 6:1
6. Employer	"Slaves, obey your earthly masters with respect and fear, and with sincerity of heart, just as you would obey Christ. . . . Masters, treat your slaves in the same way." — Ephesians 6:5, 9
7. Governmental authorities	"Everyone must submit himself to the governing authorities." — Romans 13:1–5

I described on the previous page what submission to these authorities means in brief, but let me also describe what submission *does not mean*.

Submission to authority does not necessarily mean agreement with authority. We don't have to agree with a person in authority over us in order to submit to them. If we all had to agree before we submitted, no one would ever submit to anyone else! We can always find a reason for rebellion if we're listening to our human instincts that buck against authority. But we don't have to agree with someone in order to come under them, which is a liberating reality.

Children often disagree with their parents, for example, over just about everything during some phase in their life. But parents still expect their children to follow them and come under their authority. We find a similar dynamic at play in our churches. Church leaders make decisions that don't always make sense to the people of the church, but the members are still called to follow their leaders. We follow elders, for example, because the Holy Spirit made them overseers of his church (Acts 20:28). In fact, we're even called to "obey" our leaders in the church (Heb. 13:17). Language like that can be difficult for some to accept, but we don't follow God's commands because they're easy. Nor do we have the privilege to pick and choose what makes sense to us. We follow Jesus—and come under those positions of delegated authority on earth—because Jesus is Lord. That's what we do because of who he is.

Another caveat: God never calls us to submit when our submission clearly means disobeying Scripture. God doesn't contradict himself, and we must use Scripture as our supreme guide for discerning right and wrong in life. Remember that God is above all authorities, even though he established them on earth. Scripture does not lead me to believe that God generally establishes specific individuals to authority positions; instead, the Bible speaks to how God establishes the positions of authority. This is an important distinction because individuals in authority can disobey God and sway others in their disobedience. That doesn't mean God supports that person or their leadership decisions. An individual can abuse their position of power, but that doesn't mean God supports their abuse. So even though God established their position, it doesn't mean that God appointed them to their particular role in that position. In the end, we respect the seat of authority, but if the one filling that seat asks us to do something *clearly contrary* to God's Word, we serve God not man.

As we learn to submit to God's authority properly in this world, we find it everywhere we look! So when we rebel against authority figures for unscriptural reasons, for example, we rebel against God himself. The opposite is true as well: when we submit to these authorities, we submit to God himself, in a sense.

That's the submission side of authority, but the opposite side of the coin matters too. From the beginning to the end of human history, God has invited us into his authority. God put man in control to "rule over" creation (Gen. 1:28), and, in the end, his people will receive dominion to reign with him: "They will see his face, and his name will be on their foreheads. There will be no more night. They will not need the light of a lamp or the light of the sun, for the Lord God will give them light. *And they will reign* for ever and ever" (Rev. 22:4–5; see also 5:10). God wants us to share in his reign, and unless we're submissive to God and to those in authority over us, we will never really walk in fullness. That's why submission is ultimately a gift for our good.

> God doesn't just invite us to submit to his authority; he also invites us to participate in his reign.

When submission is difficult and we struggle to remember God's good purpose in it, we can remember that God rewards those who are faithful in his kingdom in terms of power. Jesus told a parable of a king who went on a trip (Luke 19:12–27). While the king was away, he put authority in his servants' hands by giving them money: "Put this money to work . . . until I come back" (v. 13). When the king returned, he rewarded each servant according to their earnings—by giving them authority. He said to those who had doubled their money, "Take charge of ten cities," and "take charge of five cities" (vv. 17, 19). God gives authority in his kingdom when we're faithful with the lot he's assigned to us on earth. So when we work our jobs with diligence—however small our tasks might seem—God proportionately rewards us by distributing his authority to us. He calls us to submit to him, yes, but I believe ultimately that he's training us to reign with him.

Supplemental Reading

Gene Edwards's book *A Tale of Three Kings: A Study in Brokenness* (Carol Stream: Tyndale, 1992) provides a very short, imaginative retelling of the story of Saul, David, and Absalom in order to help readers understand the importance of submission to God's authorities. For those who struggle with authority, especially with spiritual authority, this book offers understanding, conviction, and hope. It's creative, engaging, and anchored in Scripture.

Submission

How are you doing with submission to God? Are you submissive to God's delegated authorities? Take stock and ask yourself with regard to each type of authority below: *Am I actively or passively resisting any of these authorities? If so, how am I acting rebelliously?*

Honestly asking these questions can feel daunting, and waiting on the true answer can feel overwhelming. Perhaps you will identify small areas of rebellion under each type. That's common, especially if this concept of submission is new to you. As you respond below, treat these areas of rebellion as possible proddings from God. Read the full passages listed in this chapter for more context surrounding the biblical commands to submit to these types of authority:

1. God himself _____

_____

2. Church leaders _____

_____

3. Believers in general _____

_____

4. Spouse _____

_____

5. Parents _____

_____

6. Employer _____

_____

7. Governmental authorities _____

_____

Your Spiritual Formation Plan

In order to focus on taking your next step, identify just one change for today: What is one way you need to repent of rebellion? Are you willing to humble yourself and change in this way? Describe your plan and ask for God's help.

15

CONFESSION

> In this chapter you will:
> - ☐ Start the habit of confessing your sins to God.
> - ☐ Identify a possible confessor (or a group) who will hear your confessions.
> - ☐ Take your next step toward regularly confessing your sins.

Just like it's not easy to serve or submit to others, confessing our sins is not easy either. But confession is good, and God forms us through this discipline. He also *frees us* through confession. Sin is a burden that we carry, and until it's off our chest, it weighs us down. As we confess, God lightens our load and renews our lives. Deep, spiritual renewal involves the confession of sin. Even our bodies can experience renewal through this practice: "Confess your sins to each other and pray for each other so that you may be healed" (Jam. 5:16).

Perhaps the greatest benefit for confessing our sins is what God does as he shapes us into the kind of persons he wants us to be. He makes us holy in the certain areas we confess, but he also makes us humbler people in general. Maximus the Confessor, the seventh-century theologian, wrote, "Every genuine confession humbles the soul." While we intuitively know that humble people confess, we must remember that people who decide to confess become humbler.

The purpose of this exercise is to help you identify someone to whom you can regularly confess your sins. But first, what is confession exactly?

> Confession is admitting out loud to God or another person our sins.

We confess our sins, and God forgives us, as Scripture says: "If we confess our sins, he is faithful and just and will forgive us our sins and purify us from all unrighteousness" (1 John 1:9). Yet sometimes we don't *feel* forgiven. That's why, I believe, God gives us the gift of confessing our sins to other people. When we speak out loud about our sins to someone in the body of Christ—and we don't get struck down by lightning right there on the spot—we feel the acceptance of God. When we are baptized into Christ, we receive salvation and a cleaned conscience. Our regular confession continues this "pledge of a good conscience toward God" (1 Pet. 3:21). It helps us accept God's forgiveness in our hearts so that his mercy feels more real to us.

We shouldn't confess our sins just to anyone, though. Our confessor—the person to whom we confess—should be reliable, humble, willing to listen, safe, not eager to "fix" us, and willing to confess their sins too. Our confessor, ideally, should also be equipped to speak the gospel over us upon our confession. Gospel-speaking means speaking out loud the Good News. When we confess our sins, our words ought to be met with the message that Jesus saves those who trust in him.

> Our confession should end with a profession that Jesus is our saving King.

Since God's grace and mercy are immense, part of God's grace in confession allows others to remind us about God's kindness toward us! We know what we've done is wrong, so we don't need to hear more about our sin. Instead, we need to be reminded of his kindness: that God loves us, wants good for us, and can help us change. A wise confessor knows that God's kindness, not his severity, leads us to repentance (Rom. 2:4).

Confession and salvation are not the end of the story, though. To make biblical confession complete, we must also repent of our sins because repentance brings about real change. The Greek word for "repentance" in the New Testament signifies a change of mind that leads to a changed life (Acts 2:38). Confession understands that while Jesus *accepts us* as we are, he doesn't *leave us* as we are. He lifts us out of the mire, sets us on our feet again, and calls us to "stop sinning" (John 5:14). Repentance is turning from our sins to live differently. So we confess our sins, but we also repent of them.

Do you have a confessor, someone who hears your confession of sin? If not, seek God and find someone to whom you can confess any and every sin at the drop of a hat. This is ideally someone within your local church. How often you confess to God depends on how often you consciously sin, and you can confess to others as often as necessary. Confession is a gift, not a once and done obligation. Both confession and repentance exist for anytime you sin, so make a regular habit of confession so that sin will not fester in the darkness

(Eph. 5:11–14). The first step, though, is to identify a trusted confessor, someone who will hear your sin and speak truth over you.

> ## Supplemental Reading
>
> John Ortberg's book *The Life You've Always Wanted: Spiritual Disciplines for Ordinary People* (Grand Rapids: Zondervan, 1997) contains a practical and helpful chapter on confession: Chapter 8, "Life Beyond Regret: The Practice of Confession." Consider also reading St. Augustine's *Confessions* (also known as *The Confessions of Saint Augustine*), which he finished writing in AD 400.

Your Spiritual Formation Plan

Use this page to take your next steps with regard to confession.

Do you regularly confess your sins to God? If not, start doing this today and make it a part of your regular prayer time.

_____

Who might regularly hear your confession? This can be a single person or a small group of trusted friends. Ask God, then jot down some ideas.

_____   _____

_____   _____

_____   _____

Of those potential confessors, to whom are you willing to confess your sins regularly? What barriers are keeping you from confessing to them?

_____

_____

_____

_____

_____

_____

_____

What's your next step toward establishing a practice of confession with them?

_____

_____

_____

_____

_____

_____

16

LISTENING

> In this chapter you will:
> - ☐ Identify a reliable guide.
> - ☐ Decide what to ask for guidance about.
> - ☐ Plan a meeting with your guide.

Each of the disciplines we covered in the last three chapters—service, submission, and confession—serves two purposes with regard to humility: they both reveal and cultivate humility in us. A fourth practice that also serves these purposes is receiving guidance *by listening*. When we actively seek wise counsel from others, we reveal existing humility and God uses that to cultivate even more humility in us.

Now, we shouldn't listen to just anyone's counsel, but only people we trust. And when we listen, we should take to heart what they say. In my experience, listening to wiser, older Christians is a vital part of our spiritual formation journey. Scripture teaches us the importance of humble listening: "The way of a fool seems right to him, but a wise man listens to advice" (Prov. 12:15); "Pride only breeds quarrels, but wisdom is found in those who take advice" (Prov. 13:10); and, "Make plans by seeking advice; if you wage war, obtain guidance" (Prov. 20:18). By heeding the guidance of wise people, we will grow and find greater success on our spiritual formation journey.

This is the last chapter of Part 2, and it serves as a reminder that our spiritual formation journey is not meant to be traveled alone. We welcome reliable guides into our lives in order to stay on track. We all need help along our journey, and listening to others is a primary way to receive help. In fact, when we refuse to listen to others, we reject God's creational intent for us.

> Listening is vital to our relational nature as humans.

God created us for relationship. That's why the Ten Commandments are all about relationships—with God and with people. The first person we listen to is God himself. This is why the *Shema* starts with "hear" in English, which comes from the Hebrew word that means "to listen and obey": "Hear [*shema*], O Israel: The Lord our God, the Lord is one . . ." (Deut. 6:4). The *Shema* goes on to describe the ways that we listen to and obey God. So while we first listen to God, God often chooses human vessels to dispel his wisdom. That's why we practice the spiritual discipline of listening to godly people for guidance. The alternative is learning the hard way, but we don't have to choose that way! God invites us to experience his grace and avoid unnecessary pain by listening to the wisdom of other believers. When you look for a wise counselor, ideally you will find someone you know and trust within your local church, such as an elder or a deacon—someone who has spiritual authority over you. But you can also find wise a counselor among friends and mentors.

I'm talking about two types of listening: listening to correction about sin and listening to wisdom about life. Both help you progress on your formation journey. A good friend or mentor will confront you about sin in your life, but here's the question: Will you receive that type of correction? A loving spouse or family member will offer feedback about how your words affect them, but will you really hear them? Truly listening is a difficult task, but humble disciples of Jesus receive "wounds from a friend" (Prov. 27:6). They know it's for their ultimate good and sanctification—and for the glory of God.

We also listen to wise counsel for direction in life. We listen to this second type of counsel differently than we listen to a rebuke because wisdom is not always about right and wrong. When it comes to hearing correction, we humbly listen and repent, but we meet wise counsel about life by weighing it in our heart. A wise spiritual mentor won't tell you what to do with your life; instead, they will serve as a sounding board for you by asking good questions and helping you make decisions. Their role is to dispel wisdom, and your role is to listen. When it comes to choosing a career, a spouse, or where to live, you might listen to the input of others, but at the end of the day, it's your decision to make.

Remember that spiritual guidance is just that—guidance. It's not spiritual mandates, dictates, or rules. A spiritual guide or counselor may offer good suggestions, but we must always take responsibility for our actions. A wise counselor once told me that it's not a mistake to make the wrong decision; the only mistake is to make the wrong decision and blame someone else for it. For all types of listening, Psalm 25:12 captures this point: "Who is the man who fears the Lord? Him will he instruct in the way that he should choose" (ESV). When we fear God, God instructs us as we choose the steps to take.

> ## Supplemental Reading
>
> Richard J. Foster's book *Celebration of Discipline: The Path to Spiritual Growth* (New York: HarperOne, 2018) contains an excellent chapter on this topic: Chapter 12, "Guidance." This book was originally published in 1978 and has stood the test of generations, yet it still carries with it a contemporary feel. I highly recommend this book as a whole, and this chapter in particular will help you learn more about the practical side of seeking guidance.

Your Spiritual Formation Plan

In the space below, consider whom you might need to listen to during this season of your life.

Who can serve as a reliable guide for you? Brainstorm below, then name only one person who is humble and can offer guidance to you. Pray about asking them to offer you guidance during this season of your life.

_____   _____

_____   _____

_____   _____

What do you want guidance about during this season of your life? Use this space to prepare for a conversation with your counselor, then set a time to meet with them.

_____

_____

_____

_____

_____

_____

_____

_____

In the next chapter, you will refine your Rule of Life. A wise counselor comes in handy at this point. As you meet with them, ask for specific feedback on your Rule of Life. Are you willing to share it with that person? Go ahead and schedule your meeting with them, but refine your Rule of Life before you meet.

17

REFINING YOUR RULE OF LIFE

In this chapter you will:
- ☐ Refine your Rule of Life.
- ☐ Celebrate your progress!

Before we continue, let me pause and congratulate you: well done! The progress you've made so far is a grace from God. And for the ways you've participated with him and responded to his promptings along the way, good work.

You've taken steps through ten core spiritual disciplines, and now you're ready to refine your Rule of Life. Consider how far you've come and what you've learned along the way. You crafted the first draft of your Rule of Life at the beginning of this workbook. Since then, you've identified your primary desire and major barriers along your journey. You also took the 21-Day Challenge to jumpstart your journey. Then, you formed your initial plan for solitude, silence, rest, reading Scripture, prayer, fasting, service, submission, confession, and listening. Your work to complete these steps will help you refine your Rule of Life.

As I mentioned at the outset, I recommend you do at least two drafts of your Rule of Life. Making changes is not only okay, but good! It means you're making progress in your plans toward becoming who you uniquely want to be in Christ. So redraft your Rule by editing and tweaking it. You can do this as many times as you see fit, until you settle on something with which you're happy. It can be something you keep for years to come, so consider it an investment of your time. While you may make additional edits after this point, go ahead and redraft it now. In the end, you should be able to measure your life with your Rule as a measuring stick.

When you are happy with it, put it somewhere you can easily access. You might even consider posting it somewhere in your home so you frequently see it. I created a Rule of Life for my family and we hung it in our room, for example,

Your Spiritual Formation Plan

to help us remember who we want to be as a family. Whatever you decide to do with your personal Rule, let it serve as a monument along the road of your spiritual formation journey.

Use the last pages of this chapter to refine your Rule of Life. But before you continue, I want to give you a vision for what's next in Part 3. My hope is that your completion of Part 1 and Part 2 has provided a launching pad for your progress, but your journey is not over yet! In Part 3 of this workbook, you will consider how to continue making plans for spiritual progress as you move beyond this initial plan.

Invite a Friend to Go Deeper
Spiritual Formation Video Course

Now that you've made important strides on your journey, consider inviting someone to walk with you as you continue. We've talked about listening to others for counsel and guidance, but don't forget that you may be that person who gives guidance to someone else!

A great way to disciple others in the disciplines is to invite them to practice the disciplines *with you*. As I mentioned at the beginning, we learn best when we marry knowledge and action. So consider inviting someone to join you in your journey—even now. You're a work in progress, but so is everyone else! And perhaps you're further along the journey than they are. One way you can invite someone to join you is by using this workbook and the class sessions that accompany this workbook in my on-demand *Spiritual Formation* video course, which you can access at himpublications.com/spiritual.

REFINE YOUR RULE OF LIFE

SPIRIT: The heart and will that form the character of my life.

MIND: The thoughts and feelings of my life.

BODY: My body, God's temple.

SOCIAL: The people in my life.

Part 3

YOUR NEXT SEASON OF SPIRITUAL FORMATION

Part 3 builds on the foundation of Parts 1 and 2 and guides you into the next season of your formation. You have your initial plan, but now is the time to settle into regular rhythms for the long-haul journey of discipleship. This part teaches you the value of a seasonal approach to spiritual formation, and it helps you form specific plans for your next season of life as well. These specific plans will launch you into forming regular spiritual habits for a lifelong journey of formation, one season at a time. Continue making progress, energized by God's grace and sustained by his mercy.

18

A SEASONAL APPROACH TO SPIRITUAL FORMATION

You took some initial steps along your spiritual formation journey, and now you're ready for what's next. Make sure to pause and thank God for what he's done in you so far because getting started is often the hardest part.

As you continue along your journey, you'll see how challenges and setbacks can be a normal part of spiritual formation. Sometimes these are unavoidable and not truly setbacks but just different legs of the journey. Challenges might come in various forms: unexpected life events, newly found weaknesses in yourself of which you were unaware, or the sheer pain of growth. Whatever your challenges, Christ can help you overcome. We have victory and power in Christ that makes possible what the apostle Peter said:

> "Grow in the grace and knowledge of our Lord and Savior Jesus Christ" (2 Pet. 3:18).

As you look forward to continued growth, I offer you an approach I've found helpful for taking a long-haul view of the disciplines: a seasonal approach to spiritual formation. This approach began for me while I was in school.

During the spring of 2010, while I was studying at Asbury Theological Seminary, author David G. Benner spoke during chapel, and his words made a profound impact on me: "The spring is always an important time for me spiritually." Before that chapel service, it had never occurred to me that our spiritual walk with God might be connected to the physical seasons of the year. But his words resonated with me, and they've continued to inform my journey even today. I've struggled with seasonal sadness during the winter months; I also feel spiritual renewal when it's warm out (especially during spring). Like Benner, I realized, the seasons affect me too, and not just my body but also my spirit. This started me thinking about spiritual formation in terms of "seasons."

In the years that followed the spring of 2010, as I experienced progress in the disciplines, I took this thought about the seasons and adopted a seasonal approach to spiritual formation. It changed the way I thought about my journey as a whole. I began thinking in terms of the literal seasons, which provided me a framework for intentionally making plans according to the four seasons of the year. I began structuring my prayer life, Scripture reading, and other disciplines into three-month segments, with mile markers set at the beginning and end of each stretch. For example, I would review my Rule of Life and start a fresh prayer list at the start of each season. And I would choose a particular book of the Bible to study.

> The seasons of the year became the primary framework around which I connected with God to organize my spiritual formation plans.

A seasonal approach to spiritual formation is when you allow your spiritual disciplines to coincide with seasonal changes. Nothing is special about the winter and summer equinoxes, nor the spring and fall solstices, but depending on my season of life, I utilize these points of time on the yearly calendar as opportunities to pause, reflect, and take stock of where I stand on my spiritual journey.

This habit of syncing my plans with the seasons began to profoundly impact me and also the group of young people I was leading at my home church. At each changing of the seasons, we gathered together in my living room and reflected on our spiritual journeys over the prior three months. We all named one thing we had learned and the one thing we wanted as we looked ahead to the coming season. This practice enabled us all to trek along together and celebrate our individual progress!

Those experiences are the genesis of Part 3 of this workbook. My goal in the remaining pages is to provide a framework to help you incorporate a seasonal approach in your spiritual formation journey. Perhaps my approach of using three months and literal seasons of the year doesn't work for you. That's okay! You can think of the term "seasonal approach" with more flexibility and apply it to metaphorical seasons of your life, however long or short they might be. A season of life for spiritual disciplines can last two months or two years. When possible, though, my recommendation is to organize your plans in the disciplines in terms of months not years. Whatever your approach, Part 3 assumes that you adopt some sort of seasonal approach that serves as a tool to help you navigate your spiritual life in this way. And I purposely designed Part 3 to mirror Parts 1 and 2 so you can pick up where you left off.

As you complete the following pages, consider what's coming in the next season of your life and move forward with confidence at what God can do in and through you. This is your opportunity to plan your next steps with God.

Righteousness builds on itself. Just like the effects of sin compound in our lives, the effects of righteousness compound too—but in the opposite direction. The more we take on the character of Christ, the more we experience growth! Learning spiritual disciplines is also cumulative, like math: each part builds on what you've covered, and it's difficult to make real progress without getting down the basics. So as we become familiar with the basics and continue to grow, we find that righteousness carries both a compounding and a cumulative effect on our lives. For example, meditation helps us pray more deeply from the heart. Finding solitude provides necessary space to hear from God in prayer. In turn, hearing from God helps us pray with more passion and earnestness. Disciplines also work in counter-cyclical ways:

> We experience how the pain of fasting meets the refreshment of rest.

They all work together in various ways as investments in our souls so we experience a spiritual sweetness that carries us deeper into the disciplines.

All along the way, your Rule of Life can serve as the compass for finding true north in your life. We know that Jesus is *the Way*, that Scripture is our final authority, and that God provides the same general pathway for all disciples. But what about *our unique journey* along the well-worn paths of righteousness? God invites each of us to walk along the Way in a *certain way* that is unique to us, our personality, and our calling.

I love the moment when Jesus spoke to Peter about his unique calling in John 21. Jesus had risen from the dead and visited some disciples on the shore of the Sea of Galilee. After they ate, Jesus was walking with Peter and said, "When you are old you will stretch out your hands, and someone else will dress you and lead you where you do not want to go" (v. 18).

Then, he said to Peter, "Follow me." At that moment, Peter turned around and saw the disciple Jesus loved following behind them. Peter said to Jesus, "Lord, what about him?" (v. 21). He wasn't sure he liked his specific calling compared to the disciple whom Jesus loved. But Jesus reminded him that Peter's lot was unique to him, and he needed to follow it:

> Jesus rebuked Peter and said, "You follow me."

God often designates certain callings on the general path of discipleship. It's important that each one of us makes space to hear from Jesus: *you* follow me. This will keep our heads straight and help us guard ourselves from comparison as we walk the straight and narrow path of life.

Your Rule of Life helps you navigate the path created by your calling. Finding your true self in Christ is the result of faithful obedience and the discovery of how to walk according to the way God has uniquely made you. You have a specific personality, a certain set of gifts, and perhaps even a particular vocational calling in life. Treasure those and cultivate them.

In order to pursue those unique elements of your walk with fervor and focused attention throughout the seasons of your life, begin each new season of your spiritual journey by reviewing your Rule of Life. Use that review process as an opportunity to reorient yourself toward being the person God calls you to be. Then, make specific plans for how you will seek God through the core disciplines, which are the means of God's grace. The pages that follow help you make those plans.

Supplemental Reading

David G. Benner's book *The Gift of Being Yourself: The Sacred Call to Self-Discovery* (Downers Grove: IVP, 2015) offers a helpful biblical theology of self-knowledge. He argues for the importance of knowing ourselves—and receiving our unique identities—in order to follow Jesus with all our beings.

19

PLANNING YOUR NEXT SEASON

In this chapter you will:
- ☐ Choose a way to mark seasons in your life.
- ☐ Use Parts 1 and 2 to plan your next season of spiritual formation.

On the following pages, you will put on paper your plans for the next season. Spiritual formation is a lifelong process, and as I suggested in the previous chapter, thinking of your spiritual formation in terms of seasons can be very helpful. Focus on the next season of your life—after you feel ready to move forward from the plan you made in Part 2—and discern the best next steps to take on your journey with God so you can cultivate a long-haul habit of making plans to mature in Christ.

Your name for the season:

Start Date:

Your Spiritual Formation Plan

Your Rule of Life

Once you've solidified your Rule of Life, review it and identify a handful of aspects you'd like to focus on during this season. Write them below. Next to each one, write an action step you can take this season to focus on that aspect.

Aspect	Action Step
_____	_____
_____	_____
_____	_____
_____	_____
_____	_____
_____	_____
_____	_____

Your Primary Desire

You may have various desires right now, but try to name your single greatest desire moving into this season of life. Remember, don't fret over whether your desire is "spiritual enough." The important task here is to be honest so you can meet God from a place of authenticity.

What is your primary desire in this season?

_____

_____

Your Greatest Challenge

Challenges always oppose your progress on your journey. Consider the events, people, and situations that will arise in the coming months, and name the single greatest challenge you will face as you seek to make spiritual progress.

What will be your greatest challenge during this season?

_____

_____

Planning Your Next Season

Your Plan for Regular Solitude and Silence

Consider where you can reliably and regularly find solitude and silence to connect with God during this upcoming season. This place should be somewhere you can be alone without interruptions or distractions. As seasons of life change, your place of solitude and silence might change. If that place has changed or needs to change, write that here.

Where will you seek regular solitude?

___

Consider new potential distractions in your life, such as new noises, interruptions, or changes caused by a change of season. Perhaps you can do something about these distractions in order to guard your time alone with God.

What do you need to do to maintain silence and avoid distractions?

___

Your Spiritual Formation Plan

As far as it depends on you, try to plan a spiritual retreat at least once a year. Go ahead and schedule this retreat, make plans for it, and communicate those plans with those who will be affected by your absence. Use the space below to sketch out your plan and make a tentative decision on the dates for your retreat.

Do you need to schedule a retreat during the coming months? If so, where will you go? What dates will you go? What preparations do you need to make now for this to go smoothly?

_____

_____

_____

_____

_____

_____

_____

Your Plan for Rest

Life and relationships change, and as they do, your habits of rest change. Consider how you will take time away from work to rest in the coming months. How exactly will you connect with God and his people through prayer and Scripture? With whom will you take a day to rest? During what time frame each week? What will you do exactly to connect with God?

What will it look like to make space for rest during this season?

_____

_____

_____

_____

_____

_____

_____

Planning Your Next Season

Your Scripture Reading Plan

Choose a companion book from Scripture for the next three to nine months. Which book of the Bible do you want to read and study this season?

_____
_____
_____

As you read from your chosen book of the Bible, specific verses might stand out to you for meditation and memorization. You can write those below over the course of your study during the coming months. Or if you want to meditate on and memorize other Scriptures, you can use the space below to plan your concentrated study of those specific passages (see Appendix C for suggestions).

_____
_____
_____
_____
_____
_____
_____
_____
_____
_____

Your Prayer List

Use the next page to begin a new prayer list for this season. Reference your initial prayer list to transfer to your new list any older items. Do you want to use the bullet-point prayer list or a day-by-day prayer list this season?

_____

PRAYER LIST

Start Date: _____

Your Fasting Plan

For this season of life, how do you want to fast? Consider how your fasting rhythm might need to change based on any life changes.

When do you want to fast regularly this season? What do you want fasting to look like in general for you during this season?

Your Plan for Cultivating Humility

The disciplines of service, submission, confession, and listening cultivate humility in us, which never changes, but how we practice them from season to season can change.

Service

Read Matthew 25:31–46 again and consider how you can focus your service this season.

- Giving food to the hungry
- Giving drink to the thirsty
- Welcoming the stranger
- Clothing the naked
- Visiting the sick
- Visiting the imprisoned

What's your plan for serving others during this season?

Submission

How are you doing with submitting yourself to God's delegated authorities in the below areas? How is God asking you to submit to these authorities during this season?

1. God himself (James 4:7)

___

2. Church leaders (Hebrews 13:17)

___

3. Believers in general (Ephesians 5:21)

___

4. Spouse (Ephesians 5:22–25)

___

5. Parents (Ephesians 6:1)

___

6. Employer (Ephesians 6:5–9)

7. Governmental authorities (Romans 13:1–5)

Confession

How's it going with your confessor? Are you regularly confessing to them? What next step do you need to take with your confessor this season?

Listening

What counsel do you need during this season? To whom can you listen? What next step do you need to take with your trusted counselor?

APPENDIX A
Rule of Life Examples

A WOMAN IN HER FIFTIES

My number-one rule of life:
In all things (words, deeds, thoughts), I will glorify God.

Spirit
- I will actively seek to fill my heart through fasting and prayer.
- I will love and serve others from the overflow of my heart.
- I will check my motives before acting (especially speaking).
- I will seek a heart of compassion.
- I will direct my strong will and determination toward seeking God's will and not my own.
- I will actively study Scripture and read reliable Christian authors.

Mind
- I will capture my thoughts and submit them to God's care and control.
- As I contemplate issues and problems, I will ask God for direction.
- I will use *Switch on Your Brain*'s process to change my thought patterns.
- I will boss my feelings around, especially with my "doing what I want to do or deserve to do" attitude.

Body
- I will consciously choose the food I put in my body.
- I will actually monitor (via annual lab work), listen to, and pay attention to my body and how well it is functioning, and then make adjustments.
- I will not eat processed foods.
- I will strenuously exercise three times per week and regularly exercise two to three times per week for a total of five to six times per week.
- I will look for variations of exercise to improve upper body strength, flexibility, and better balance.

Social

- I will be a soft place to land for hurting people.
- I will seek and foster relationships that glorify God.
- I will seek opportunities to expand my casual social circles to give opportunities for God to shine through me.
- I will lead with transparency and trust in relationships.

A MAN IN HIS THIRTIES

My number-one rule of life:

I will always be an authentic person of integrity when in front of people and when alone.

Spirit

- I will do everything from a place of honoring God.
- I will confess my sins to God *and* to another brother in the faith *daily*.
- I will make sure to be spiritually fed weekly by someone else so that I'm being led and not always the one leading. This could be done through media (video, movie, book, podcast) or a person in my life.
- I will create space weekly to individually connect emotionally with my family.

Mind

- I will pause daily and appreciate something beautiful that God has made—Scripture, nature, art, people.
- I will meditate on Scripture every single day, at least seven minutes.
- I will remind myself with Scripture that no matter how I feel or think, I am a child of God and he is faithful to his word.
- I will read a little bit of really good fiction every day.
- I will journal every week on what's going on in my head.
- I will go to counseling again, if only for six-month checkups.
- I will watch a great film/TV show every week.
- Everything I create will be at a level that represents the creator of creativity.

Body

- I will work out three times a week, for at least ten minutes.
- I will do yoga three times a week.

Appendix A

- I will learn to be a decent builder and handyman to provide for my family.
- I will limit the fast food that enters my body to two times per week.
- I will be active with my kids every day.

Social

- I will spend time weekly with close friends.
- I will always be discipling someone.
- I will always have a close mentor in my life.

APPENDIX B
How to Do a Book Study

*Do your best to present yourself to God as one . . .
who correctly handles the word of truth.*

— 2 Timothy 2:15

This appendix outlines two types of book studies: a simple and detailed version. If possible, do your book study in community with at least one other person, and if you have access to a trained Bible teacher, process your findings and conclusions with them.

OPTION 1: SIMPLE BOOK STUDY

You can conduct a simple book study in three steps: 1) read the book once to get the big picture, 2) read the book again and write down themes from the book, then 3) read the book a third time to decide the main theme.

OPTION 2: DETAILED BOOK STUDY

The following five steps outline a detailed way to conduct a book study:

1. Prepare for Reading
2. Identify the Theme
3. Make Structural Divisions
4. Conduct a Word Study
5. Exegete and Apply

Your Spiritual Formation Plan

Step 1. Prepare for Reading

> *Your preparation will help you make good use of your time as you proceed.*

- ☐ Prayerfully choose a book of the Bible you want to study.
- ☐ Get a copy of the book you can write on. If possible, print out a copy of the book. Consider obtaining a "raw" version of it, with no section titles, chapters, or verses by using biblegateway.com or a comparable source.
- ☐ Select a notebook or a journal where you can keep a running tab of your observations and questions as you do this book study.

Step 2. Identify the Theme

> *It's important to identify the primary theme of the book you're studying because this helps you understand from a high level what's happening in the details.*

- ☐ Read through the entire raw version of your chosen book in one sitting.
    - ☐ As you read, keep a running tab of your questions and observations.
    - ☐ List potential book themes as you read. While you are reading, ask yourself and the Holy Spirit, *What are some of the main emphases in this piece of literature?*
- ☐ You may want to read the book multiple times until you can identify potential themes.
- ☐ Identify what you think is the main theme of the book. You may need to read it again to identify from the themes you listed what is the primary theme—the one that stretches the entire document.

Step 3. Make Structural Divisions

> *Dividing your book into parts helps you see the flow and progression of the book. Once you make the divisions, focus on just one subsection of your book. You will use this subsection for conducting a word study in Step 4.*

Appendix B

a. Make Section and Subsection Divisions

> *Section divisions are three to five parts of your book, and subsection divisions are three to five parts of your sections. Results vary from person to person how to divide a certain book into parts, so don't worry about finding the "one way" to do this. Your divisions serve as a tool to help you better understand the macro-view in its major parts.*

- ☐ Read the whole book again, still in raw format, dividing it into three to five major sections. Do this with your printed-out version that has no chapters, verses, or headers, using a pencil to divide the book into sections.
- ☐ Then, scanning the book as a whole, divide each of the three to five major sections you created into three to five subsections:
    - ☐ Make a chart that shows your sections and subsections (see the example below). While you will mark the divisions on your raw copy, use a Bible with chapters and verses so you can write the exact citations for the sections and subsections of your chart.
    - ☐ Label each section and subsection with a name you choose that represents those verses by topic.

Example Structure of Matthew

PROLOGUE 1:1–25	The Reign of God: Jesus' Ministry to the Sheep of Israel 2:1–18:35			The Reign of God: Jesus' Ministry in Jerusalem 19:1–28:15		COMMISSION 28:16–28:20
	His Ministry Begins 2:1–4:16	His Fame Spreads: He Preaches, Heals, and Exorcizes 4:17–9:38	His People Learn Their King 10:1–18:35	The Vineyard of the King 19:1–20:34	Victory in the City of the King 21:1–28:15	

119

b. Focus on One Subsection

> *Subsection divisions help you focus on a particular passage of the Bible. You are now ready to understand the parts in light of the whole! The parts then give you more insight into the book as a whole as well.*

- ☐ Read slowly through your subsection, writing your questions and observations.
- ☐ Read through the subsection again to identify a few topics that interest you.
- ☐ From this subsection, select one to three verses that are the most interesting, confusing, or convicting to you personally.
- ☐ Write down as many observations and questions about your verse(s) as possible.
- ☐ Make a few conclusions about what you think your passage says about God, people, and obedience based on the immediate context of your subsection and the book as a whole.

Step 4. Conduct a Word Study

> *A word study helps you understand the meaning of a word in the Bible as used by your author in your particular book. The meaning of words is contextual, so a word study gives you a practical way to understand how that word is used in a particular context by looking at its meaning in various contexts.*

- ☐ Chose a prominent, interesting, or rare word from the one to three verses you focused on from your chosen subsection.
- ☐ Study that word using an online tool like *Bible Gateway* (biblegateway.com) or *Blue Letter Bible* (blueletterbible.org).
- ☐ Using one of those online tools, search for all occurrences of your word in the Bible. Once you identify all the verses in the Bible, read them through in one sitting to get the general sense of how the word is used and take notes as you go. The goal here is to form categories of how various biblical writers use this word in context.
- ☐ As you read, take notes on 1) what you're observing about that word, 2) what categories of meaning exist in the Bible outside your particular book, and 3) anything else important to you.
- ☐ Summarize your conclusions in one paragraph.

Appendix B

- ☐ Write another paragraph to apply your general conclusions about this word to your particular passage, using the immediate context to discern how it's being used in that instance.

Step 5. Exegete and Apply

> *Exegesis means to "draw out" meaning from Scripture. This is deciding what message the author intended the original audience to understand. Exegesis provides meaning; application provides the significance of that meaning for our world today. Step 5 helps you find both the meaning and significance of your passage.*

- ☐ Write between 250 and 300 words that include these elements:
  - ☐ "Their Town."* Determine the meaning of your one to three verses, using 1) your word study, 2) your subsection study, and 3) your understanding of the theme of the book as a whole.
  - ☐ Crossing the "Principlizing Bridge." Answer the question: *What is your primary takeaway?*
  - ☐ "Own Town." Apply the meaning to our world today.
  - ☐ Your life. In one sentence that begins with "I will . . ." answer the question: *What is God asking me to do as a result of this study?* If God speaks, listen and obey.
- ☐ Process your study with a trusted mentor, teacher, or fellow student of the Word. As you do, ask them what they think as you:
  - ☐ Explain to them your process.
  - ☐ Tell them about your observations and questions.
  - ☐ Show them your structural and subsection divisions chart.
  - ☐ Tell them about your word study.
  - ☐ Share with them your exegesis and application.
  - ☐ Then, ask them these three questions to end:
    - ○ Have I missed anything?
    - ○ Is my application in line with God's Word as a whole and with wisdom?
    - ○ What else would you add?

---

*The language of "Their Town," "Principlizing Bridge," and "Our Town" comes from J. Scott Duvall and J. Daniel Hays's book *Grasping God's Word* (page 179).

Supplemental Reading

For more information on the Inductive Bible Study method, see David R. Bauer, *Inductive Bible Study: A Comprehensive Guide to the Practice of Hermeneutics* (Grand Rapids: Baker Academic, 2014). This resource provides insight into the theoretical foundations behind this method in general, along with practical guidance on conducting a book study in particular.

Another useful tool I recommend is J. Scott Duvall and J. Daniel Hays's book *Grasping God's Word: A Hands-On Approach to Reading, Interpreting, and Applying the Bible*, second edition (Grand Rapids: Zondervan, 2005). This book provides a solid introduction to hermeneutics, including a thorough explanation on how to read a book of the Bible in context. It's an excellent resource to help readers understand how to make connections between the ancient cultures of the Bible and our world today.

APPENDIX C
Key Scripture Verses for Memorization

As you make your plan for Scripture reading, select some passages for memorizing. Below is a list of passages I suggest everyone memorize. These are some of the most important passages of the Bible, and they uniquely capture the heart of God. While I recommend memorizing the entirety of these passages, memorize any part of these as you see fit.

- Genesis 12:1–3
- Exodus 19:4–6
- Deuteronomy 6:4–9
- Joshua 1:9
- Psalm 1
- Psalm 23
- Proverbs 3:5–6
- Isaiah 61
- Jeremiah 31:31–34
- Matthew 5–7
- Matthew 28:18–20
- Luke 15:1–32
- John 10:10
- John 13–17
- Acts 20:18–35

Pick at least six verses from this list to start (e.g., Gen. 12:1–3; Exod. 19:4–6), and commit to memorizing those verses during the next three months. Write down the date you plan to finish memorizing these passages as part of your plan in the chapter of this workbook called "Reading Scripture."

By picking a goal date, you can track your progress! This exercise will help you learn how to memorize Scripture so this can become a life-long habit.

Meditating on and memorizing Scripture is one of the most elemental and important parts of your spiritual formation plan. Do not skip this important aspect of your growth. Few people take the time to memorize God's Word because the thought is, *I can just look it up!* But that misses the point of memorization. Knowing how to find something is different than transformational knowing. Learning God's Word in our hearts allows for a type of knowledge that transforms our minds and impacts our lives.

NOTES

In the introduction of this workbook, the quote about making plans comes from *The Spirit of the Disciplines*, published in 1988 by HarperCollins (page 13). In the chapter "Crafting Your Rule of Life," I adapt my definitions for terms—spirit, mind, body, and social—from Willard's *Renovation of the Heart*, published by NavPress in 2002. Chapter 2, "The Heart in the System of Human Life" (pages 27–44). In "Introducing the Disciplines," the Dallas Willard quote about grace, effort, and earning comes from page 34 of *The Great Omission* (published by HarperCollins in 2006). In the same chapter, I adapted the core disciplines list from Chapter 9, "Some Main Disciplines for the Spiritual Life," of Willard's *The Spirit of the Disciplines* (page 158).

The quote in "Solitude" about solitude being the "most fundamental" discipline of abstinence is from *The Spirit of the Disciplines* (page 161). In my discussion about when to fast in "Fasting," I reference the early Christian practice of fasting. This comes from *Didache* 8, "Concerning Fasting and Prayer." I mention in the "Service" chapter that humility is the second-most prized virtue in the New Testament. This comes from Jerry Bridges's assessment of love and humility in his book *The Blessing of Humility*, published by NavPress in 2016 (page xi). The quote in "Confession" from Maximus the Confessor comes from *Philokalia* in the section "Various Texts on Theology, the Divine Economy, and Virtue and Vice Third Century" (paragraph 62).

ABOUT THE AUTHOR

CHAD HARRINGTON leads Harrington Interactive Media and HIM Publications. Having earned degrees in biblical studies from Ozark Christian College and Asbury Theological Seminary, he's passionate about making the church more beautiful. He and his wife, Rachel, live with their children in Franklin, Tennessee.

Printed by Libri Plureos GmbH in Hamburg, Germany